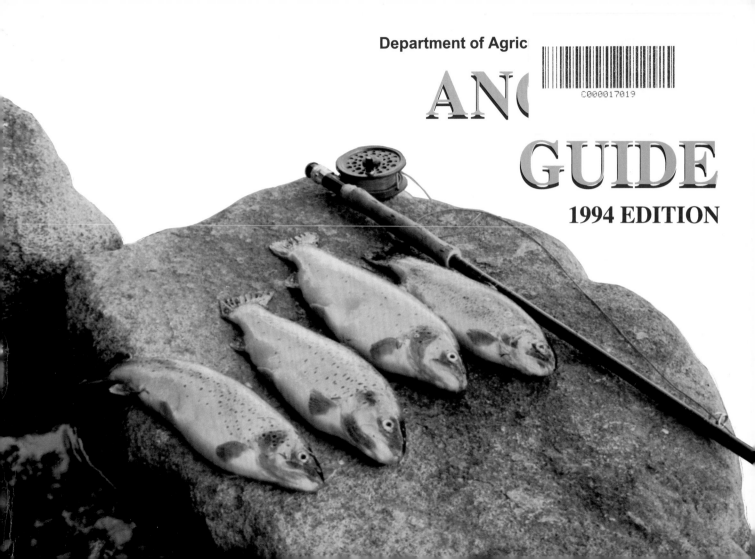

Acknowledgements

The photographs reproduced in this publication were supplied by:-

Department of Agriculture staff

Front cover photograph by Christopher Hill Photography – *(Stoneyford Reservoir, Co Antrim).*

Compiled by Fisheries Division.

Designed by DANI Communications Unit.

Printed in the United Kingdom for HMSO

Dd.8402402   C.70   55-9744   11/93

CONTENTS

CONTENTS

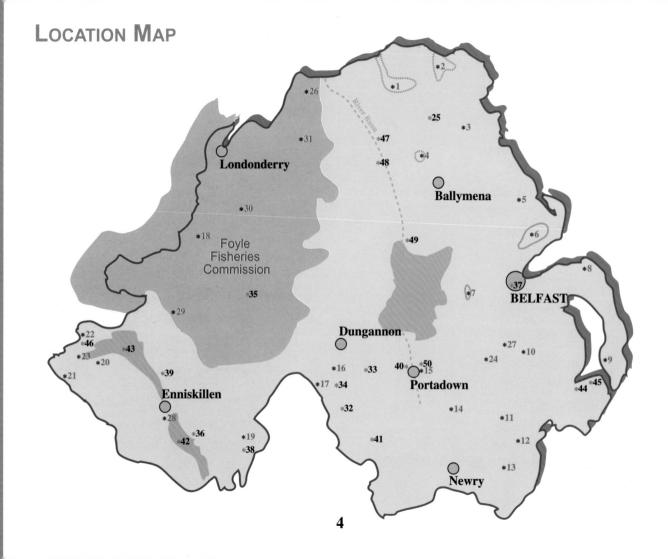

GAME WATERS

*1 River Bush
*2 Margy/Carey/Glenshesk Rivers
*3 Dungonnell Reservoir
*4 Maine Angling Waters
*5 Killylane Reservoir
*6 Woodburn Reservoirs and Lough Mourne
*7 Stoneyford and Leathemstown Reservoirs
*8 Portavoe Reservoir
*9 Lough Cowey
*10 Ballykeel Lougherne
*11 Castlewellan Lake
*12 Shimna River
*13 Spelga Reservoir
*14 Lough Brickland
*15 Craigavon City Park South Lake
*16 Brantry Lough
*17 White Lough
*18 River Mourne
*19 Loughs Corry and Corranny
*20 Navar Forest Lakes
*21 Lough Melvin
*22 Lough Keenaghan
*23 River Erne (Belleek)
*24 Lagan River (Iveagh)
*25 Altnahinch Reservoir
*26 Binevenagh Lake

*27 Hillsborough Lake
*28 Mill Lough (Bellanaleck)
*29 Loughs Braden and Lee
*30 Loughs Ash and Moor
*31 River Roe

MIXED AND COARSE WATERS

*32 Enagh Lough
*33 Blackwater River
*34 Creeve Lough
*35 River Strule
*36 Colebrooke River
*37 Lagan River (Belfast)
*38 Mill Lough (Killyfole)
*39 Ballinamallard River
*40 Upper River Bann (Portadown)
*41 Clay Lake
*42 Upper Lough Erne
*43 Lower Lough Erne
*44 Quoile Basin and River
*45 Lough Money
*46 Lough Scolban
*47 Movanagher Canal
*48 Portna Canal
*49 Toome Canal
*50 Craigavon City Park North Lake

LOCATION MAP

THE GUIDE TO FISHERIES CONTROLLED BY THE DEPARTMENT OF AGRICULTURE FOR NORTHERN IRELAND

INTRODUCTION

The Angling Guide provides anglers with a wealth of useful information in a compact form. Produced by the Department of Agriculture for Northern Ireland (DANI), it forms a comprehensive summary of the Department's fisheries and is based on the position at the date of publication. The Guide has been compiled with both local anglers and visitors in mind and it is hoped that it will encourage more anglers to enjoy the wide variety of excellent fishing available.

This edition is designed to make information as easily accessible as possible to both local and visiting anglers. The information on each water and the maps have been updated and clarified, and a *How to Get There* section for each water gives clear directions on how to find even the most remote water.

The Fisheries Act (NI) 1966 gave the Department of Agriculture responsibility for the acquisition and development of public angling waters. Today there are some 64 waters developed for public use. These include 31 still water game fisheries with a total area of approximately 1,057 hectares (2,625 acres) and 11 stretches of game fishing rivers, which total over 82 kilometres (51 miles) in length. For coarse fishing there are 7 lakes with a total area of 211 hectares (528 acres) and 6 stretches of river and canal fishing totalling 31.5 kilometres (19 ½ miles). In addition, Upper and Lower Lough Erne provide a further 15,254 hectares (37,800 acres) of mixed game and coarse fishing, and there are 4 other lakes with a total area of 81 hectares (203 acres) and 3 stretches of river totalling 15.3 kilometres (9 ½ miles) which also provide mixed game and coarse fishing.

Lough Erne is world-famous for coarse angling. The world record for a five-hour match has been broken on four different occasions there. As well as the better known match fishing stretches of Cornagrade, Broadmeadow, Sillees, Ring and Queen Elizabeth Road, there are numerous smaller less well-developed areas where pleasure fishing can be enjoyed. Lower Lough Erne is also a renowned trout fishery where fish of up to 7.7 kg (17 lb) have been taken.

International coarse fishing matches have also been held on the Upper River Bann at Portadown, where Hoy's Meadow and the Boulevard Stretch have provided record-breaking catches.

The Department provides good salmon angling on the Rivers Bush, Roe, Mourne and Shimna. Additional day tickets, bookable in advance, are required for the four restricted salmon stretches on the downstream stretches of the Bush and for the Shimna. These are available at a reduced price to holders of Department of Agriculture Game Fishing Permits.

A wide diversity of trout waters is available throughout Northern Ireland and anglers may fish for brown and rainbow trout in rivers, loughs and put-and-take fisheries. Some rainbow trout waters are open throughout the year and other waters are reserved for the fly fishing specialist.

Shimna River

7

ACCESS TO PUBLIC FISHERIES

To provide public fisheries, the Department has made numerous agreements with riparian owners (those who own the land bordering a lake or river) which are subject to the angler respecting and protecting the owners' property and interests. It is especially important not to block gates, other access roads and narrow country lanes. In the past, the abuse of riparian property has resulted in the closure of several popular angling waters in Northern Ireland. Please remember that your Department Permit only gives you permission to fish, not to abuse others' property, nor to jeopardise the angling facilities enjoyed by many people.

LITTER

As in many other public places, the problem of litter on Department waters is increasing. In addition to bags, bottles and cans it is now not unusual to find many other unsavoury items! Litter is not only ugly, it is a health hazard to both humans and wildlife.

Landowners take a serious view of litter, as broken glass, plastic bags and hooks and pieces of fishing line can endanger livestock. If the problem is bad enough, they can, and will, refuse to allow anglers access to the fishery. In addition, where the litter problem is at its worst, especially around public reservoirs, the Department may have to consider closing fisheries.

We know that the majority of anglers do not cause the litter, but you are urged to take home your own litter, and to dispose correctly of other people's litter. By doing this you will be making a very positive contribution towards the preservation of our countryside and fisheries.

PLEASE RESPECT THE COUNTRYSIDE AND FOLLOW THE COUNTRY CODE

STOCKING

The stocking policy of the Department is designed to meet the angling demand that exists in Northern Ireland. A regular census of usage is carried out on many Department waters which allows an estimate of angling demand to be made. This measure of demand is then correlated with the basic environmental and productivity information which is maintained for each fishery to decide the stocking level of each water.

The major problem that the Department has encountered is the uneven demand for its waters. For example, in the Greater Belfast Area, with its high angler population, demand is nearly ten times greater than elsewhere in Northern Ireland. Obviously, catch rate suffers and can be as low as one takeable fish every eight hours compared to the more normal demand waters which have an average catch rate of one takeable fish every three or four hours.

The refinement and improvement of the stocking programme depends on the accuracy of the census returns. Anglers using Department waters are therefore encouraged to provide accurate information to our census takers and to provide any other relevant information directly to Fisheries Division.

MOVANAGHER FISH FARM

Movanagher Fish Farm was established in 1968 to supply the Department's fisheries with brown and rainbow trout. It occupies a one hectare (2½ acre) site about 3.2 km (2 miles) north of Kilrea on a narrow strip of land between the River Bann and the navigational canal which takes river traffic past the Movanagher weir.

At present around 500,000 brown trout and 200,000 rainbow trout are grown for stocking out as takeable sized fish, or as 15 cm (6 inch) fingerlings which will grow to takeable size in about a year. The majority of these are stocked in Department waters, but some are available for angling clubs and other private sales.

In addition, brown trout are used for the reinstatement of fish populations in rivers after drainage works and fish kills due to pollution. Much of this work is done using eyed ova and fry.

The Senior Fisheries Officer with responsibility for angling development, who is based at Movanagher, and the Fish Farm Manager, are both available to advise anyone considering setting up put-and-take fisheries, and angling clubs, either on stocking levels for their waters, or on setting up club hatcheries to enhance their own waters.

Visitors are always welcome at the fish farm, and if a few days notice of the visit is given, guided tours can be arranged. Perhaps the best time to visit is from around the middle of November to February, when the broodfish are stripped. Juvenile fish can be seen at all times and visitors may feed them with food which will be supplied at the farm.

RIVER BUSH SALMON STATION

The River Bush is managed as a premier game fishery by the Department of Agriculture's Fisheries Division. Together with the provision of a high quality game fishery, the River Bush Salmon Station services the River Bush Salmon Project, a programme of inter-related scientific projects concerned with the ecology and conservation biology of Atlantic salmon.

This programme of research is essentially long-term in nature, largely as a consequence of the long life cycle of Atlantic salmon. The necessary base-line data, on which the success of the research programme depends, is derived from fish counts obtained from the operation of a number of specially designed fish traps which intercept smolts (juvenile salmon migrating to the sea) and adults returning to their home river to spawn.

Broodstock fish selected from returning adult spawners provide ova for the hatchery. These hatchery-reared ova and fry are used for stock enhancement and reinstatement in the River Bush and other DANI waters, such as the Blackwater and the Lagan. They are also used for ranching, where the ova are reared to pre-smolt stage and tagged prior to release to the sea. In addition, surplus ova may be sold to angling clubs for stocking their waters, and to other bodies, both within and outside Northern Ireland. This research programme has led to the recognition of the River Bush as an "index river" by the International Council for the Exploration of the Sea (ICES). The River Bush has been designated to provide long-term scientific information to ICES, whose concept states, "Specific rivers should be selected and monitored over a long period to provide information on annual smolt production, exploitation rates, geographical distribution of catches, adult returns, and spawning escapement".

Through its pioneering work on the River Bush, DANI is proud to have provided a lead to the international scientific community in the field of salmon fishery modelling and assessment.

Visitors are always welcome at the Salmon Station, and if a few days notice of the visit is given, guided tours can be arranged. Perhaps the best time to visit is around the middle of February, when the broodfish are stripped. Juvenile fish can be seen at all times, and visitors may feed them with food which will be supplied at the Salmon Station.

REGULATIONS

Fishing regulations are standardised as far as possible and it is intended to keep changes to a minimum. However, if any changes occur before the next revision of the Angling Guide these will be published in the annual supplement to the Guide and also in press releases to the local newspapers.

Copies of statutory regulations are available from the Government Bookshop, 80 Chichester Street, Belfast BT1 4JY.

Anyone who contravenes the regulations is guilty of an offence and is liable to be prosecuted.

METHODS, RESTRICTIONS ETC.

Permitted methods of angling, duration of season, size and bag limits, etc, are detailed on the relevant page for each water.

Anglers are reminded that lead shot is poisonous to wildlife, and are advised to use one of the modern alternatives.

The use of gaffs is illegal in the Fisheries Conservancy Board area.

Definitions for the different methods of angling and related terms, as laid down in the Angling (Department of Agriculture Waters) Bye-laws are as follows:-

"all lawful methods" means any method of angling with rod and line, except a method forbidden by any statutory provision for the time being in force;

"fly fishing" means the use of a single rod, reel (including a fixed spool reel), fly line or blow line and a single cast carrying not more than three artificial or winged natural flies, but does not include the use of a bubble float in conjunction with artificial or winged natural flies;

"ground bait" means any material used other than on a hook and designed for the purpose of attracting fish to a natural or artificial bait;

"maggots" means any larvae of the house-fly of the Genus *Musca* and the blue-bottle or blowfly of the Genus *Calliphora* and any other insect larvae of the Order Diptera;

"shrimp fishing" means the use of a single hook baited with a shrimp *(Crangon* species);

"spinning" means the use of a single rod, reel (including a fixed spool reel) and line to cast or throw an artificial or natural bait and retrieve the bait by rewinding the line onto the drum of the reel with the bait kept in motion throughout;

"trolling" means the drawing of a fishing line, with one or more hooks attached, through the water from a moving boat;

"worm fishing" means the use of a single hook baited with one or more earthworms *(Lumbricus* species).

LICENCES AND PERMITS

Anglers are sometimes confused about the difference between a licence and a permit. A licence is required by law for each fishing rod used by anyone over 18 years of age to fish anywhere in Northern Ireland (except for sea angling). Under the age of 18, a rod licence is required only if game fishing in the Foyle area. Licences are issued by either the Fisheries Conservancy Board (FCB) or the Foyle Fisheries Commission (FFC) depending on which area you are fishing in (see map on page 4).

The FCB and FFC are conservation bodies responsible for protecting fish stocks in Northern Ireland. Both bodies issue angling licences in their respective jurisdictions and, on payment of a supplement, licence holders are allowed to fish in the other's jurisdiction.

A permit is a separate document issued by the owner of a fishery which confers the right to fish in that fishery. An owner can be a private individual or company, an angling club or a government department.

It should be noted that both the rod licence and Department permit entitle the holder to use one rod only. A separate licence and permit is required for each additional rod used. A juvenile using more than one rod for either game or coarse fishing requires a full adult licence and permit for his second and every subsequent rod.

Details of the licences and permits required to fish Department waters are listed on the relevant page for each water.

The following licences are currently available from the FCB:

Game fishing

Season game fishing rod licence

8-day game fishing rod licence

One-day game fishing rod licence

Endorsement to Foyle Fisheries Commission season game fishing rod licence

Joint licence/Department of Agriculture permit (8 days)

Coarse fishing

Season coarse fishing rod licence

8-day coarse fishing rod licence

Joint licence/Department of Agriculture permit (8 days)

Joint licence/Department of Agriculture permit (3 days)

NOTE: Game fishing licences also cover coarse fishing.

The following licences are currently available from the FFC:

Game fishing

Season game fishing rod licence

14-day game fishing rod licence

1-day game fishing rod licence

Under 18 years of age game fishing rod licence

Endorsement to Fisheries Conservancy Board season game fishing rod licence

Licences are not required for coarse fishing in the FFC area.

The following permits are currently available, conferring the right to fish on Department of Agriculture (DANI) waters:

Game fishing

General season game fishing permit

Juvenile (under 18) season game fishing permit

8-day general game fishing permit

Daily general game fishing permit

Local season game fishing permit

Disabled anglers' season game fishing permit

Coarse fishing

Annual general coarse fishing permit

NOTE: Game fishing permits also cover coarse fishing.

Under the age of 18 a coarse fishing permit is not required.

The charges for licences and permits are usually adjusted annually and published in the supplement to the Angling Guide. Supplements are obtainable free of charge from distributors of Department of Agriculture permits, or from Fisheries Division.

Distributors for rod licences and Department permits have been appointed throughout Northern Ireland. Names and addresses of local distributors are listed in the supplement. Most types of permits and licences can be obtained from any of these listed distributors.

Local permits

The Department provides Local Game Fishing Permits for anglers who wish to confine their sport to a local area. These are annual permits which cover named game waters in the area for which the permit is valid. However, in addition to these waters, holders may fish on all Department coarse fisheries. The following list shows the game and mixed fisheries which are available under each local permit:-

Name of local permit	Waters covered
East Antrim	Upper South Woodburn, Lower South Woodburn, Middle South Woodburn, North Woodburn, Lough Mourne and Copeland (Marshallstown) Reservoirs
North Antrim	Killylane, Dungonnell and Altnahinch Reservoirs, River Bush (unrestricted stretch), Margy, Carey and Glenshesk Rivers
South Antrim/ North Down	Stoneyford, Leathemstown and Portavoe Reservoirs, Hillsborough Lake and Ballykeel Lougherne

Armagh/Tyrone	Craigavon City Park South Lake, Brantry Lough, Lough Brickland, White Lough and River Blackwater	**West Fermanagh**	Lough Melvin, Lough Keenaghan, Navar Forest Lakes (Achork, Meenameen and Glencreawan) and River Erne
South Down	Lough Brickland, Castlewellan Lake, Spelga Reservoir, Quoile Basin and River, and Shimna River	**Londonderry/Tyrone**	Binevenagh Lake, Loughs Ash, Moor, Braden and Lee and River Roe
East Fermanagh	Corranny and Corry Loughs, Upper and Lower Lough Erne, Mill Lough (Bellanaleck), Colebrook River		
Mid Fermanagh	Mill Lough (Bellanaleck), Upper and Lower Lough Erne, Ballinamallard River (Riversdale) and River Erne		

Permits and Licences Required for GAME FISHING on DANI Waters

The following chart has been prepared to assist anglers, especially those new to the sport and visitors to Northern Ireland, to decide which licence and permit is most suitable for them.

Regular Angler *Fishing all season throughout Northern Ireland*	**Regular Angler** *Fishing all season but restricted to local area*	**Visiting/Occasional Angler**	**Anglers under 18 years of age**
Season Game Fishing Rod Licence - FCB for main area of NI: FFC for Foyle Area	Season Game Fishing Rod Licence - FCB or FFC depending on which area to be fished	8-Day Game Fishing Rod Licence - FCB 1-Day Game Fishing Rod Licence - FCB 14-Day Game Fishing Rod Licence - FFC 1-Day Game Fishing Rod Licence - FFC	No Rod Licence required for FCB area FFC under 18 Game Fishing Rod Licence
DANI General Season Game Permit (covers all DANI waters in NI)	DANI Local Season Game Permit	DANI - 8-Day General Game Fishing Permit DANI Daily (1-day) Game Fishing Permit Combined 8-day Game Fishing Rod Licence (FCB) and DANI Permit	DANI Juvenile Season Game Permit

Regular Angler	Visiting/Occasional Angler	Anglers under 18 years of age
Season Coarse Fishing Rod Licence - FCB No Coarse Rod Licence required for Foyle Area DANI Annual Coarse Fishing Permit	8-Day Coarse Fishing Rod Licence - FCB Combined 8-Day Coarse Fishing Rod Licence (FCB) and DANI Permit Combined 3-Day Coarse Fishing Rod Licence (FCB) and DANI Permit	No Licence or Permit required

NORTHERN IRELAND SCHOOLS' COARSE FISHING COMPETITION

Every year the Department organises the Northern Ireland Schools' Coarse Fishing Competition. It is sponsored by Shakespeare Company (UK) Ltd, the Northern Ireland Tourist Board and the Ulster Coarse Fishing Federation. All secondary level schools are invited to enter teams of four pupils in the competition, and over 300 children take part each year. Recently the competition has been divided into two sections – Junior and Senior, with shields and videos for winning teams and individual prizes of fishing tackle.

The Department appreciates the co-operation of schools in the successful staging of this competition which plays an important part in the Department's policy to encourage an awareness of the sport among young people.

PRIVATE FISHERIES

Some private fishery owners, including a number of angling clubs, issue permits to visitors. See *Angling Club Waters Available to the Public* on page 144, and *Private Fisheries Available to the Public* on page 153.

FREE FISHERIES

A number of so-called 'free' fisheries are available to the public. These are mostly coarse fishing waters in County Fermanagh and no Department permit is required. However, anglers using these waters must hold the appropriate rod licence and obtain the permission of riparian landowners to cross their land. Details of these fisheries may be obtained from Department of Agriculture, Fisheries Division.

FACILITIES FOR DISABLED ANGLERS

It is suggested that disabled anglers will find the following waters particularly accessible, and special facilities are provided in some cases:-

COUNTY ANTRIM

Lower Bann Navigational Canal - Movanagher
- Three fishing stands have been provided near the car-parks.

River Bush - Day Ticket Stretches - Town Stretch
- Access for wheelchairs has been provided from the car-park to the Bridge Pool.

Killylane Reservoir
- Good access but margins may be soft in wet weather.

River Lagan (Belfast)
- Good angling access from the tow-path, but there is a steep slope at the Sharman Road entrance.

Woodburn Reservoirs
- North Woodburn is accessible, but not particularly safe.
- Middle South has access to the water at the upper end. DOE Water Executive, Milebush Service Station will provide a key for the gate. The reservoir is a considerable distance from the car-park.

COUNTY ARMAGH

Upper Bann River

- Some stands suitable for wheelchair users have been provided at the Council Stretch of Hoy's Meadow. Keys for the gate are available from Eden Villa, Bachelors Walk, Portadown BT63 5BQ, telephone: (0762) 330003.

Craigavon City Park Lakes

- There is a slipway for launching non-mechanical boats, which is readily accessible.

COUNTY DOWN

Castlewellan Lake

- A disabled anglers' car-park has been provided near the lake, and shore fishing from the boating steps and south bank is possible.

Hillsborough Lake

- Access to the fishery from the perimeter path is good.

Portavoe Reservoir

- There are several suitable places for disabled anglers at the north-east end.

Quoile Basin

- A special disabled anglers' car-park provides good access to the fishing and amenity centre. Several special stands have been built. Keys are available from the Quoile Countryside Centre, 5 Quay Road, Downpatrick, (telephone (0396) 615520).

COUNTY FERMANAGH

Lower Lough Erne
- There is good access at Stewarts Shore, and limited access from Ely Lodge, Boa Island Bridges, Muckross and Trory.

Upper Lough Erne
- There is good access at Broadmeadow and Cleenish Island.
A disabled anglers' fishing stand has also been erected at Corradillar near the Lady Craigavon Bridge. A key is available at the Share Centre, Lisnaskea, Co Fermanagh, (telephone (03657) 22122).

River Erne
- There is limited access via the public access points.

Corrany
- Although the banks may be weedy, wheelchair access is usually possible.

Lough Melvin
- There are accessible launching points for disabled anglers who can use boats.

Mill Lough (Bellanaleck)
- There is limited access, but one fishing stand for a wheelchair is available at Stevenson's House.

COUNTY LONDONDERRY

Binevenagh Lake
- Access is possible, but there are no protective barriers.

River Roe
- There is a car-park and access for wheelchairs to the right bank.

22

COUNTY TYRONE

Lough Bradan
- There is disabled and wheelchair access around the entrance road and car-park.

Moor Lough
- A surrounding gravel road gives easy access to all the shoreline.

River Mourne
- There is access at Sion Mills and the Sion Mills Angling Club should be contacted for further information.

White Lough
- There is limited access at the car-park. Unfortunately, the angling stands are not accessible for wheelchairs.

DISABLED ANGLERS' PERMIT

The Department has introduced a special fishing permit for disabled anglers who are in receipt of one of the following allowances:
– Disability Living Allowance
– Attendance Allowance
– War Disablement Pension
– Severe Disablement Allowance.
It is available only from Fisheries Division, Hut 5, Castle Grounds, Stormont, Belfast BT4 3PW.
Application forms are available from distributors. The permit is valid for all Department waters, including coarse fisheries.

FACILITIES FOR DISABLED ANGLERS

WHO TO CONTACT

SUBJECT	CONTACT	TELEPHONE NO.
Angling Permits, Permits, General Information, Enquiries, etc	Department of Agriculture Fisheries Division Hut 5, Castle Grounds, Stormont, Belfast BT4 3PW	Belfast (0232) 520100 Ext 23434 or 23431 Fax (0232) 761327
Development of Angling Waters	Movanagher Fish Farm 152 Vow Road, Ballymoney, Co Antrim BT53 7NT	Kilrea (02665) 40533
Salmon Research, Booking of Bush Day Tickets	Bushmills Salmon Station, Church Street, Bushmills, Co Antrim BT57 8QJ	Bushmills (02657) 31435
Rod Licences, Commercial Fishing Licences, Pollution, Bailiffing, Poaching, Illegal Fishing	Fisheries Conservancy Board (FCB) 1 Mahon Road, Portadown, Craigavon, Co Armagh BT62 3EE	Portadown (0762) 334666
	Foyle Fisheries Commission (FFC) 8 Victoria Road, Londonderry BT47 2AB	Londonderry (0504) 42100

TALKS ON FISHERIES

The Department's technical staff are willing, subject to other commitments, to meet groups of anglers or others interested in fisheries or fisheries management, and to give short talks or participate in discussions.

Applications should be made well in advance to the Chief Fisheries Officer at the Department of Agriculture, Fisheries Division.

LOCAL FISHERIES OFFICES

Fisheries Office,
Crown Buildings,
The Mall West,
Armagh BT61 9BL

Armagh (0861) 522774
Fax (0861) 523889

Fisheries Office,
Riversdale,
Ballinamallard,
Co Fermanagh

Ballinamallard
(0365) 388529

Fisheries Office,
River Bush Salmon Station,
Church Street,
Bushmills,
Co Antrim BT57 8QJ

Bushmills
(02657) 31435
Fax (02657) 32130

Fisheries Office,
Castlewellan Forest Park,
Castlewellan,
Co Down BT31 9BU

Castlewellan
(03967) 78937

Fisheries Office,
Ravarnet House,
Altona Road,
Lisburn,
Co Antrim BT27 5QB

Lisburn
(0846) 661615
Fax (0846) 661619

Movanagher Fish Farm,
152 Vow Road,
Ballymoney,
Co Antrim BT53 7NT

Kilrea (02665) 40533
Fax (02665) 41307

LIST OF DEPARTMENT OF AGRICULTURE WATERS

Water	Type of Fishing	Season	Fly Fishing Only	Boats Permitted	Page
Achork	Still - Game	C	From boats	Yes	116
Altnahinch	Still - Game	E	No	No	32
Ash	Still - Game	D	No	No	136
Ballinamallard	River - Mixed	E	No	No	94
Ballykeel Lougherne	Still - Game	C	Yes	No	70
Bann - Lower	Canal - Coarse	A	No	No	34
Bann - Upper	River - Mixed	Coarse A Game C	No	No	58
Binevenagh	Still - Game	B	No	No	122
Blackwater	River - Mixed	Coarse A Game C	No	No	62
Bradan	Still - Game	D	No	No	128
Brantry	Still - Game	C	Yes	Yes	130
Brickland	Still - Game	C	Yes	No	72
Bush	River - Game	D	Partly	No	36 & 40
Carey	River - Game	C	Partly	No	50
Castlewellan	Still - Game	C	From boats	Yes	74
Clay	Still - Coarse	A	No	No	64
Colebrook	River - Coarse	A	No	No	96
Copeland	Still - Game	C	No	No	54
Corranny	Still - Game	C	No	No	108
Corry	Still - Game	C	From boats	Yes	108
Cowey	Still - Game	A	Yes	Yes	76

See page 28 for key to seasons

Water	Type of Fishing	Season	Fly Fishing Only	Boats Permitted	Page
Craigavon North	Still - Coarse	A	No	Yes	66
Craigavon South	Still - Game	B	No	No	66
Creeve	Still - Coarse	A	No	Yes	132
Dungonnell	Still - Game	C	No	No	42
Enagh	Still - Coarse	A	No	No	134
Erne (Upper & Lower)	Still - Mixed	Coarse A	No	Yes	98
		Game E	No	Yes	
Erne	River - Game	E	From boats	Yes	104
Glencreawan	Still - Game	C	From boats	Yes	116
Glenshesk	River - Game	C	No	No	50
Hillsborough	Still - Game	B	No	No	78
Keenaghan	Still - Game	C	Yes	Yes	106
Killyfole	Still - Coarse	A	No	No	108
Killylane	Still - Game	C	Yes	No	44
Lagan (Belfast)	River - Coarse	A	No	No	46
Lagan (Iveagh)	River - Game	E	Partly	No	80
Leathemstown	Still - Game	C	No	No	52
Lee	Still - Game	D	No	No	128
Lower South Woodburn	Still - Game	C	Yes	No	54
Maine	River - Game	F	No	No	48
Margy	River - Game	C	Partly	No	50
Meenameen	Still - Game	C	From boats	Yes	116

See page 28 for key to seasons

continued overleaf

LIST OF DEPARTMENT OF AGRICULTURE WATERS

Water	Type of Fishing	Season	Fly Fishing Only	Boats Permitted	Page
Melvin	Still - Game	G	No	Yes	112
Middle South Woodburn	Still - Game	C	No	No	54
Mill (Bellanaleck)	Still - Game	C	Yes	Yes	114
Money	Still - Coarse	A	No	No	82
Moor	Still - Game	D	No	No	136
Mourne Lough	Still - Game	C	No	No	54
Mourne	River - Game	F	No	No	138
Navar Forest Lakes	Still - Game	C	From boats	Yes	116
North Woodburn	Still - Game	B	No	No	54
Portavoe	Still - Game	C	Yes	No	84
Quoile	River - Mixed	Coarse A Game C	No	No	86
Roe	River - Game	F	No	No	124
Scolban	Still - Coarse	A	No	Yes	118
Shimna	River - Game	C	No	No	88
Spelga	Still - Game	C	No	No	90
Stoneyford	Still - Game	C	No	No	52
Strule	River - Coarse	H	No	No	140
Upper South Woodburn	Still - Game	C	Yes	No	54
White	Still - Game	B	From boats	Yes	142

Seasons

A All year

B 1 February–31 December

C 1 March–31 October

D 1 March–20 October

E 1 March–30 September

F 1 April–20 October

G 1 February–30 September

H 21 October–30 June of following year

KEY TO MAPS

━━━━━━━━━━ Main road

────────── Minor road

━━━━━━━━━━ River or canal

▬▬▬▬▬▬▬▬ Department stretch

++++++++++++++++ Railway line

················· International border

Loughs, lakes, reservoirs and sea

Forest area

Car-parks

County Londonderry

County Antrim

County Tyrone

County Fermanagh

County Armagh

County Down

29

Upper South Woodburn Reservoir

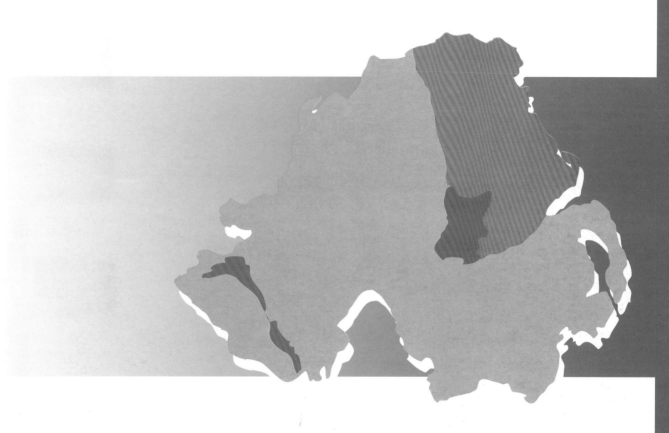

ALTNAHINCH RESERVOIR

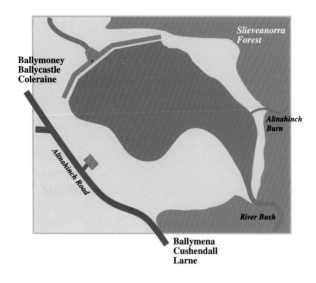

Nearest Town	- Ballymoney
Area	- 17.8 hectares (44 acres)
Species	- Brown trout and rainbow trout
Season	- 1 March–30 September
Methods	- Fly fishing, spinning and worm fishing
Bag Limit	- 4 fish per rod per day
Size Limit	- Minimum takeable size 25.4 cm (10 inches)
Other Restrictions	- None
Boats	- Fishing from boats is not permitted
Licence	- *Over 18* - Fisheries Conservancy Board Game Fishing Rod Licence
	- *Under 18* - None
Permit	- *Over 18* - Department of Agriculture Game Fishing Permit
	- *Under 18* - Department of Agriculture Juvenile Game Fishing Permit.

Note: This is a public reservoir and care should be taken not to cause pollution.

Altnahinch Reservoir, at the head of the River Bush, is situated in an exposed area of peaty moorland, although much of the surrounding area has been forested. The banks are fairly solid and ideal for shore fishing. The bay at the head of the reservoir can be quite sheltered and has a deep channel which can be easily covered from the south-western shore.

There is a native stock of free-rising brown trout but this has been supplemented with an initial stocking of takeable size fish from Movanagher Fish Farm and will be topped up throughout the season. The Department's Agriculture and Environmental Sciences Division is carrying out stock density experiments with juvenile salmon in the feeder streams and some land-locked salmon have been sighted in the reservoir. Test nettings of the reservoir have revealed trout in excess of 2.25 kg (5 lb).

HOW TO GET THERE

From Ballymena (23.5 km - 14½ miles) take the A43 (Glenarriff Road) to Martinstown. Turn left at the crossroads, fork right after 1.5 km (1 mile) to Newtown Crommelin. Turn right then left at the staggered crossroads and continue for 4 km (2½ miles). Turn left onto the Altnahinch Road. The reservoir is on the right 3.2 km (2 miles) from the junction.

From Ballymoney (21.3 km - 13¼ miles) take the B16 through Kilraghts. At the end of the road turn left onto the A44. Take the second right in the Drones to Ballyhoe Bridge. Turn right, then fork left and then right just before Knocklavrinnen Bridge onto the Altnahinch Road. The reservoir is on the left 5.6 km (3½ miles) from the junction.

COUNTY ANTRIM

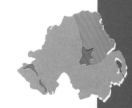

LOWER BANN NAVIGATIONAL CANAL
TOOME, PORTNA AND MOVANAGHER

(Designated Coarse Fisheries)

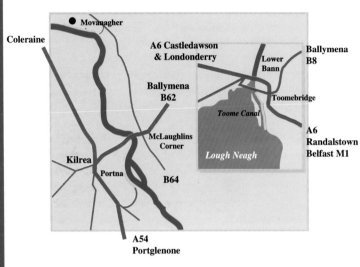

Nearest Towns	- Toomebridge (Toome stretch), Kilrea (Portna & Movanagher stretches)
Length	- Toome 0.8 km (½ mile) Portna 0.4 km (¼ mile) Movanagher 1.6 km (1 mile)
Species	- Pike, perch, roach, bream and eels
Season	- All year round
Methods	- All lawful methods including ground bait and maggots for coarse fish
Bag Limit	- 2 pike per day
Size Limit	- Pike of 4 kg (8.8 lb) and over must be returned to the water
Other Restrictions	- See following notes
Boats	- Fishing from boats is not permitted
Licence	- *Over 18* - Fisheries Conservancy Board Coarse Fishing Rod Licence - *Under 18* - None
Permit	- *Over 18* - Department of Agriculture Coarse Fishing Permit - *Under 18* - None.

These canal stretches are all readily accessible and are popular coarse fisheries. Pike, perch, roach, bream and eels are abundant.

The lower part of the Toome stretch is noted for perch. Fishing at Portna is restricted to the stretch below the locks. Upstream of the locks is inaccessible and dangerous due to the precipitous nature of the rocky banks. Note that car-parking is not permitted on the canal bank road at Movanagher and fishing is not allowed from the west or middle bank between the canal and the river. Two car-parks have been provided at the canal bank.

For the disabled, three fishing stands have been erected at Movanagher. These stands are adjacent to car-parks, one of which is the fish farm car-park.

HOW TO GET THERE

Toome - travelling from Randalstown and Belfast on the A6 towards Londonderry take the first or second street to the left in Toome village.

Portna - off the A54 Kilrea-Portglenone road 0.4 km (¼ mile) out of Kilrea turn left for a short distance and left again to the canal area.

Movanagher - from Kilrea by the B64 signposted towards Ballymoney for 2.4 km (1½ miles) over the Bann Bridge to McLaughlin's corner. Here turn left and immediately left again and travel for 3.6 km (2¼ miles) to the approach road to Movanagher Fish Farm on the left.

A touring caravan site is available at Bracknamuckly Wood, Portglenone Forest.

COUNTY ANTRIM

RIVER BUSH - DAY TICKET STRETCHES

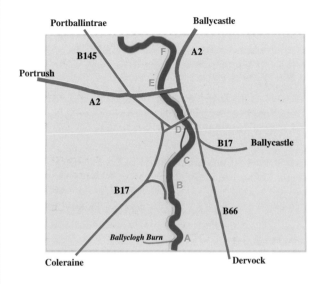

Portballintrae Ballycastle
B145
Portrush
A2
B17 Ballycastle
B17
B66
Ballyclogh Burn
Coleraine Dervock

A–B Walk Mill Stretch
B–C Leap Stretch
C–D No Fishing
D–E Town Stretch
E–F New Stretch

Day tickets are available for four stretches of water at Bushmills which can accommodate up to 15 rods per day.

Nearest Town - Bushmills

Length - Town Stretch - 180 metres (200 yards)
New Stretch - 457 metres (500 yards)
Leap Stretch - 560 metres (620 yards)
Walk Mill Stretch - 686 metres (750 yards)

Species - Salmon, sea trout, brown trout, steelhead trout

Season - 1 March–20 October

Methods - Fly, worm and shrimp permitted at all times
Spinning is not permitted when the red section is visible on the marker posts erected at the head of each stretch
Prawns, maggots and ground bait may not be used

Bag Limit - None

Size Limit - All trout under 25.4 cm (10 inches) in length, and all juvenile salmon, must be returned unharmed to the water

Other Restrictions-

- Except for the Town Stretch, fishing is from the west (left-hand) bank only
- The day ticket is not transferable
- The day ticket is valid only on the date stated between 8 am and one hour after sunset or 10 pm, whichever is the earlier. Tickets issued for half-day fishing are valid on the date stated between either 8 am and 2 pm (morning fishing) or 2 pm and one hour after sunset or 10 pm, whichever is the earlier (evening fishing)
- The catch return on the reverse of the day ticket must be completed and returned to the booking office permit box on completion of fishing
- All fin-clipped fish (those from which the adipose fin has been removed) must be submitted to the hatchery office for examination on the day on which they are caught, or for fish caught outside office hours or at weekends or public holidays, as soon as possible on the next working day
- All foul-hooked fish must be returned gently to the river

- The day ticket, game rod licence and DANI permit (if applicable), must be produced when requested by an authorised officer of the Department of Agriculture and/or the Fisheries Conservancy Board for Northern Ireland
- The day ticket may be forfeited if the holder acts contrary to any of these conditions or commits any breach of the Fisheries Act, Bye-laws or Regulations
- The Department reserves the right not to issue day tickets to any person who has breached the day ticket conditions

Town Stretch - 3 rods (half-days available 1 June to 20 October)
New Stretch - 3 rods
Leap Stretch - 6 rods (half-days available 1 June to 20 October)
Walk Mill Stretch - 3 rods

RIVER BUSH

Boats   - Fishing from boats is not permitted

Licence   - *Over 18* - Fisheries Conservancy Board Game Fishing Rod Licence
- *Under 18* - None

Permit   - *Over 18* - Department of Agriculture Game Fishing Permit (General Season Game, Local Season Game, 8-Day Game)
- *Under 18* - Department of Agriculture Juvenile Season Game Fishing Permit.

Note: It is not essential to have a DANI permit. Anglers without a DANI permit pay a higher day ticket charge.

Ticket -

Day tickets are available from the booking office at the River Bush Salmon Station in Bushmills, and should be booked in advance. Anglers are advised to use the postal pre-booking system. Note that early application is necessary for peak times (especially March, July and September). Weekend and public holiday angling must be booked and the tickets paid for by 2 pm on the preceding Friday or normal working day. Tickets will not be issued until they are paid for.

Tickets bearing details of catches (nil or otherwise) must be returned to the booking office permit box before leaving.

The River Bush Game Fishery is an integral part of an experimental salmon river which is managed primarily for ecological research studies into the life cycle of Atlantic salmon. However, within the terms of the research programme, game angling of the highest quality is made available to the public.

The co-operation of anglers is essential because the success of the research project depends on the accuracy of the record of each year's total run of fish, which, of course, includes the rod and line catch. Day tickets must be returned with the catch return on the reverse side completed, even when this is nil return. Anglers are asked to submit all salmon which have been caught downstream of the Salmon Station (Town and New Stretches) for examination and scale sampling, during office hours if possible. A cash reward is given for scale samples obtained.

It is very important for the research staff to examine fin-clipped fish (those from which the adipose fin has been removed) as they normally contain tiny tags which can only be detected using specialised equipment. These fish will be returned to anglers immediately after examination, and a reward is given for the retrieval of the tags. Any angler catching a fin-clipped fish outside office hours or at weekends and public holidays is asked to retain the head and bring it to the Salmon Station as soon as possible. The angler should indicate on the catch return that a fin-clipped fish has been caught.

Angling on the river has been divided into several stretches to give the best sport possible and to cater for varying desires. The river is a 'flash spate' water and does not remain in top class order for extended periods. When in form, however, it provides excellent sport. There are named pools on each of the day ticket stretches, and anglers are expected to move from pool to pool.

HOW TO GET THERE

From Ballymoney, either take the B66 to Bushmills through Dervock, turn left over the bridge in Bushmills, and left again into the Salmon Station; or, take the B62, through Ballybogey for 11 km (7 miles). Turn right onto the B17 to Bushmills. Turn right into Bridge Street and right again just before the bridge into the Salmon Station.

From Portrush take the A2 to Bushmills. Turn right after the school at the T-junction into Priestland Road, and first left after St Cuthbert's RC Church into Bridge Street. Turn right just before the bridge into the Salmon Station.

Directions to the stretches are available from the booking office in the Salmon Station.

COUNTY ANTRIM

RIVER BUSH – UNRESTRICTED STRETCH

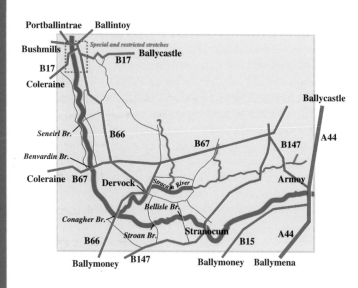

Nearest towns	- Bushmills, Dervock, Armoy
Length	- 38.5 km (24 miles)
Species	- Salmon, sea trout, brown trout
Season	- 1 March–20 October
Methods	- Fly fishing only 1 March–30 June
	Fly fishing, spinning and worm fishing from 1 July
	Spinning and worm fishing from Bellisle Bridge to Conagher Bridge and on the Stracam tributary up to Dervock is also permitted from 1 July
Bag Limit	- None
Size Limit	- Minimum takeable size for brown trout is 25.4 cm (10 inches)
Other Restrictions	- A short stretch above Benvardin Bridge is closed to anglers due to the close proximity of the Lion Park
Boats	- Fishing from boats is not permitted
Licence	- *Over 18* - Fisheries Conservancy Board Game Fishing Rod Licence
	- *Under 18* - None

Permit   - *Over 18* - Department of
                 Agriculture Game Fishing Permit
              - *Under 18* - Department of
                 Agriculture Juvenile Game
                 Fishing Permit.

The unrestricted stretch of the Bush offers the chance of a good day's sport in a variety of delightful settings. From the downstream limit at Ballyclogh Burn to Stroan Bridge the river is mainly slow moving and fairly deep with isolated fords, and flows between high banks. From Stroan Bridge to Magherahoney the pace of the river quickens and faster flowing water over gravel begins to predominate. However, there are deeper pools and a fair chance of making contact with a good salmon. The brown trout fishing is also of a high order and some stocking takes place every year to supplement this.

Above Magherahoney the river changes to a mountain stream with water cascading over large boulders and small but deep pools with extensive bush cover. The chance of a salmon in this reach is much diminished but there is a good stock of small brownies and on the right day the sport can be fast and furious.

Anglers are asked to complete a catch return which can be obtained from the booking office at the Bush Salmon Station.

HOW TO GET THERE

Access to the river is best gained from one of the many bridges or official car-parks. These are signposted and the angler should have no difficulty in locating them. Some of the main bridges and access roads are listed below:

Benvardin Bridge - on the B67 between Ballycastle
                       and Coleraine
Dervock   - on the B66 between Ballymoney
                       and Bushmills
Armoy   - on the A44 between Ballymena
                       and Ballycastle
Stranocum Bridge- on the B147 between Ballymoney
                       and the B67.

Access along the river bank has been made easier by the construction of stiles and foot sticks over most of the distance between the downstream limit and Armoy. However, anglers are reminded of the Country Code and are asked to respect it.

COUNTY ANTRIM

DUNGONNELL RESERVOIR

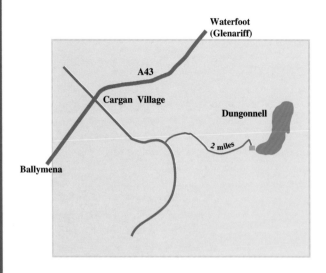

Nearest Town	- Ballymena
Area	- 28 hectares (70 acres)
Species	- Brown trout
Season	- 1 March–31 October
Methods	- Fly fishing, spinning and worm fishing
Bag Limit	- 4 fish per rod per day
Size Limit	- Minimum takeable size 25.4 cm (10 inches)
Other Restrictions	- None
Boats	- Fishing from boats is not permitted
Licence	- *Over 18* - Fisheries Conservancy Board Game Fishing Rod Licence
	- *Under 18* - None
Permit	- *Over 18* - Department of Agriculture Game Fishing Permit
	- *Under 18* - Department of Agriculture Juvenile Game Fishing Permit.

Note: This is a public reservoir and care should be taken not to cause pollution.

This long and narrow reservoir lies in wind-swept moorland on the upper reaches of the Clough River. The shores near the dam are rocky and very good for shore fishing. On the south side the shore is firm for most of the distance, but the west shore is more marshy as you go eastward and care should be taken. The peninsula on the north side just above the dam gives a pleasant variation with a sheltered bay in the lee side.

The reservoir contains native brown trout from the inlet spawning streams. However, past angling returns indicated a high proportion of undersized fish, and the natural stock is now supplemented with takeable sized fish from Movanagher Fish Farm.

Both touring and long stay caravan sites are available at nearby Glenariff Forest Park.

HOW TO GET THERE

Take the A43 (Waterfoot and Cushendall) from Ballymena. Turn right at the crossroads just as you approach Cargan, about 16 km (10 miles) out of Ballymena. The road to the reservoir is signposted 0.8 km (½ mile) from Cargan.

Take to the woods

Forest Service

Department of Agriculture for Northern Ireland Forest Service, Room 38, Dundonald House, Belfast BT4 3SB. Tel (0232) 524949

COUNTY ANTRIM

KILLYLANE RESERVOIR

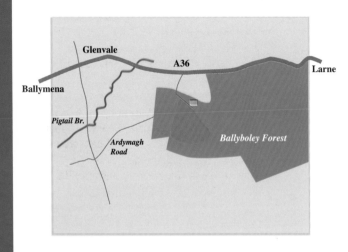

Nearest Town	- Larne
Area	- 20 hectares (50 acres)
Species	- Brown trout
Season	- 1 March–31 October
Methods	- Fly fishing
Bag Limit	- 4 fish per rod per day
Size Limit	- Minimum takeable size 25.4 cm (10 inches)
Other Restrictions	- None
Boats	- Fishing from boats is not permitted
Licence	- *Over 18* - Fisheries Conservancy Board Game Fishing Rod Licence
	- *Under 18* - None
Permit	- *Over 18* - Department of Agriculture Game Fishing Permit
	- *Under 18* - Department of Agriculture Juvenile Game Fishing Permit.

Note: This is a public reservoir and care should be taken not to cause pollution.

KILLYLANE RESERVOIR

This reservoir is situated on open moorland but the planting of conifers around the lake has provided some shelter.

The banks are open and there are no access problems at normal water levels, but care must be taken when areas of mud are exposed under low water conditions.

Killylane contains a plentiful stock of wild brown trout which is supplemented by stocking. This maintains good fishing throughout the season.

A touring caravan site is available nearby in Ballyboley Forest.

HOW TO GET THERE

From Ballymena or Larne – entrance by the main reservoir gates on the south side of the main Ballymena-Larne Road, the A36, 20 km (12½ miles) from Ballymena, 11.25 km (7 miles) from Larne.

The main gates are closed between 10 pm and 8.30 am in summer, or the hours of darkness in winter. Alternative access is from the Ardymagh Road – about 1.6 km (1 mile) on the Ballymena side of the reservoir, turn south at the crossroads at Glenvale. Cross the Pigtail Bridge and turn left at the crossroads onto the Ardymagh Road.

RIVER LAGAN

(Designated Coarse Fishery)

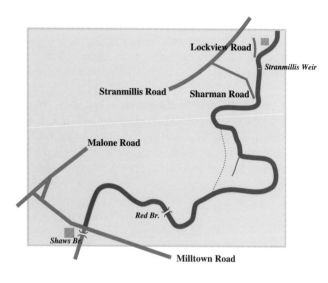

Nearest Town	- Belfast
Length	- 9 km (5½ miles)
Species	- Roach, perch, rudd, gudgeon, bream and pike
Season	- All year
Methods	- All lawful methods including ground bait and maggots
Bag Limit	- 2 pike per day
Size Limit	- Pike of 4 kg (8.8 lb) and over must be returned to the water
Other Restrictions	- None
Boats	- Fishing from boats is not permitted
Licence	- *Over 18* - Fisheries Conservancy Board Coarse Fishing Rod Licence
	- *Under 18* - None
Permit	- *Over 18* - Department of Agriculture Coarse Fishing Permit
	- *Under 18* - None.

This stretch of the River Lagan has improved greatly over recent years due to the improvement in water quality. Fishing points are available all along the old tow-path which is on the west side of the river from the Red Bridge downstream to Stranmillis Weir and beyond. Access will be improved by the Laganside development as far down as the Queen's Bridge.

SALMON IN THE LAGAN

Over the past three years the Department's scientists have restocked tributaries with salmon fry in an experiment to assess whether the improvement in water quality would allow the return of adult fish. In 1993 over 35 fish were taken by rod and line from the river. Game anglers require a Game Angling Licence and Permit. This is a developing fishery and the Department intends to add further stocks of fish as the quality continues to improve.

HOW TO GET THERE

Shaws Bridge is on the Belfast Ring Road between Newtownbreda (Supermac Shopping Centre) and the Malone Road. The Red Bridge is a short distance downstream.

The Stranmillis Weir is reached from Lockview Road or Sharman Road, both off the Stranmillis Road.

COUNTY ANTRIM

47

RIVER MAINE

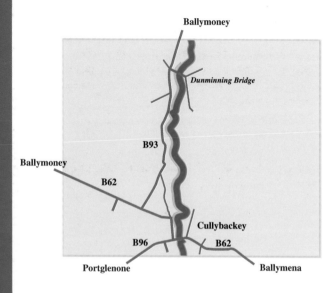

Nearest Town	- Cullybackey
Length	- 6.5 km (4 miles)
Species	- Salmon, brown trout
Season	- 1 April–20 October
Methods	- Fly fishing, spinning and worm fishing, but spinning is not permitted in April, May and June
Bag Limit	- 6 fish
Size Limit	- Minimum takeable size 23 cm (9 inches)
Other Restrictions	- No Sunday fishing
Boats	- Fishing from boats is not permitted
Licence	- *Over 18* - Fisheries Conservancy Board Game Fishing Rod Licence
	- *Under 18* - None
Permit	- Maine Angling Club Daily Permit.

Under an agreement with the Department of Agriculture, Maine Angling Club issues up to 12 daily permits to people wishing to fish on their stretch of the river. This extends (with a few exceptions) to about 6.5 km (4 miles) of fishing from both banks of the river from a point a few hundred yards above Cullybackey to just beyond Dunminning Bridge.

The river varies greatly over this comparatively short length with interesting pools and runs available for both fly and worm fishing. Spinning is not permitted in the months of April, May and June. There is an excellent head of hard fighting native brown trout which average 0.25 kg (½ lb) but which can grow considerably larger and there is also the added attraction of dollaghan (big Lough Neagh trout) up to 2.25 kg (5 lb) and salmon in the later months of the season.

Daily permits (except Sunday) can be obtained from Simpson's Newsagent, Pottinger Street, Cullybackey. The day permit distributor is normally closed on bank and public holidays but opens until 10 am to sell permits to visiting anglers. The responsibility rests with the angler to ensure that he or she is in possession of a permit before starting to fish.

HOW TO GET THERE

Cullybackey is on the B62 Ballymena to Kilrea Road, 4.8 km (3 miles) from Ballymena.

COUNTY ANTRIM

MARGY, CAREY AND GLENSHESK RIVERS

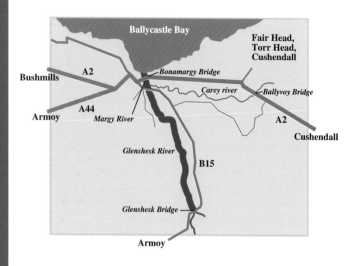

Nearest Town	- Ballycastle
Length	- Margy 0.8 km (½ mile) Carey 3.6 km (2¼ miles) Glenshesk 5 km (3 miles)
Species	- Salmon, sea trout and brown trout
Season	- 1 March–31 October
Methods	- Margy River - fly fishing only between Bonamargy Bridge and the confluence of the Carey River. Fly fishing, spinning and worm fishing on the remainder. Carey and Glenshesk rivers - fly fishing, spinning and worm fishing
Bag Limit	- None
Size Limit	- None
Other Restrictions	- No digging for bait
Boats	- Fishing from boats is not permitted
Licence	- *Over 18* - Fisheries Conservancy Board Game Fishing Rod Licence - *Under 18* - None
Permit	- *Over 18* - Department of Agriculture Game Fishing Permit - *Under 18* - Department of Agriculture Juvenile Game Fishing Permit.

The Margy River and tributaries are noted sea trout fisheries with a run of salmon late in the season.

Fishing on the Margy is almost entirely from the right bank by agreement with the riparian owner, Ballycastle Golf Club. Anglers should therefore have particular regard to golfers' interests and be alert to the cry of 'fore' which means a golf ball is flying dangerously near! On certain days each year, during competitions, fishing from the golf course will be restricted. Notices will be posted.

HOW TO GET THERE

The Margy runs into the sea at Ballycastle, which is on the A2 between Cushendall and Bushmills.

ANGLING SAFETY TIPS

LIVE TO FISH ANOTHER DAY
LEARN TO SWIM — LEARN LIFE-SAVING

When bank fishing: Avoid weak and crumbling banks.

When wading: Know the underwater geography of the area; avoid underwater cliffs and slopes; avoid soft areas of mud.

When boat fishing: Use a sound, suitable boat and equipment; wear a life-jacket; check the weather forecast; do not wear waders or gumboots; do not overload the boat; do not stand upright to play and net fish; move carefully to avoid capsizing.

Children: Teach them water safety; watch them when around water.

WHEN ANGLING — THINK SAFETY

COUNTY ANTRIM

STONEYFORD AND LEATHEMSTOWN RESERVOIRS

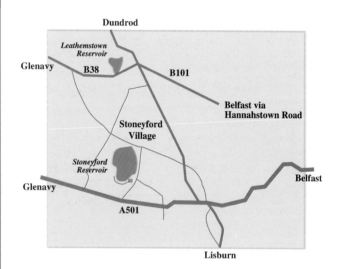

Nearest Town	- Lisburn
Area	- Stoneyford 65 hectares (160 acres) Leathemstown 11.3 hectares (28 acres)
Species	- Brown and rainbow trout
Season	- 1 March–31 October
Methods	- Fly fishing, spinning and worm fishing
Bag Limit	- 4 fish per rod per day
Size Limit	- Minimum takeable size 25.4 cm (10 inches)
Other Restrictions	- No digging for bait Angling is not permitted before 8 am nor later than 10 pm
Boats	- Fishing from boats is not permitted
Licence	- *Over 18* - Fisheries Conservancy Board Game Fishing Rod Licence - *Under 18* - None
Permit	- *Over 18* - Department of Agriculture Game Fishing Permit - *Under 18* - Department of Agriculture Juvenile Game Fishing Permit.

Note: These are public reservoirs and care should be taken not to cause pollution.

Anglers must use the official entrances and on no account trespass on the adjoining lands. Unless a special reason exists, cars should be parked only in the car-parks so that the adjacent roads are not obstructed. Wading is permitted but care should be taken as it may be dangerous when the water is at certain levels.

Stoneyford is one of the most popular Department fisheries, and is stocked regularly with takeable sized fish from Movanagher Fish Farm.

HOW TO GET THERE

From Belfast to Leathemstown via the B38 Hannahstown Road off the Falls Road, towards Glenavy for 14.5 km (9 miles). There is a fishery sign at the crossing with the B101.

From Belfast to Stoneyford via the A501 Glen Road 13 km (8 miles) to Sales Corner turning right at B101 towards Dundrod for 1.2 km (¾ mile), then left at the signpost for Stoneyford. The reservoir is signposted on the left.

Via the M1 leaving at the Moira roundabout by the A26 towards the airport. Turn left into Glenavy on the A26 going through the village and taking the B38 towards Belfast. Leathemstown is on the left 3.5 km (2½ miles) out. For Stoneyford, fork right off the B38 at the 'Y' bridge 4.4 km (2¾ miles) out of Glenavy. The reservoir is on the right after passing Stoneyford village.

From Belfast International Airport via the A26 towards Belfast to the Nutts Corner roundabout taking the B101 towards Lisburn through Dundrod. Leathemstown is on the right 2.4 km (1½ miles) past Dundrod. The signpost for Stoneyford is 5.6 km (3½ miles) past Dundrod.

COUNTY ANTRIM

WOODBURN RESERVOIRS

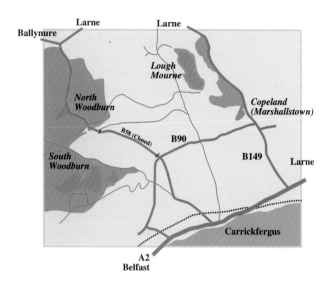

Nearest Town - Carrickfergus

Area - Upper South 26.5 hectares (65 acres)
Middle South 25.9 hectares (64 acres)
Lower South 9 hectares (22 acres)
North 7 hectares (18 acres)
Lough Mourne 51 hectares (127 acres)
Copeland (Marshallstown) 9.7 hectares
(24 acres)

Species - North - Rainbow trout
Others - Brown and rainbow trout

Season - North - 1 February–31 December
Others - 1 March–31 October

Methods - Upper and Lower South - Fly
fishing
Others - Fly fishing,
spinning and worm fishing

Bag Limit - 4 fish per rod per day

Size Limit - Minimum takeable size 25.4 cm
(10 inches)

Other Restrictions- No digging for bait
Angling is not permitted before
8 am nor later than 10 pm

Boats - Fishing from boats is not
permitted

Note: These are public reservoirs and care should be taken not to cause pollution.

Licence	- *Over 18* - Fisheries Conservancy Board Game Fishing Rod Licence
	- *Under 18* - None
Permit	- *Over 18* - Department of Agriculture Game Fishing Permit
	- *Under 18* - Department of Agriculture Juvenile Game Fishing Permit.

Wading is permitted but care should be taken as this can be dangerous when the water is at certain levels. Anglers must use the official entrances and on no account trespass on adjoining lands or park their cars in such a way as to obstruct roadways or gate entrances.

These are very popular lakes and are stocked regularly with takeable sized fish from Movanagher Fish Farm.

HOW TO GET THERE

From Belfast – all the reservoirs are approached by the M5 and A2 towards Carrickfergus.

Upper, Middle and Lower South: As you go into Carrickfergus take the B58 towards Ballynure. About 1.6 km (1 mile) out (at the Brown Cow Inn sign) fork left for 0.4 km (¼ mile) to cross the B90 at Woodburn village. Carry on past the B90 for 2.4 km (1½ miles), over the hump-back bridge to the lane on the left at the Waterworks dwelling.

North Woodburn: Take the B58 from Carrickfergus towards Ballynure. The reservoir is to the left of the road after 5.6 km (3½ miles).

Copeland: Through Carrickfergus on the A2 towards Whitehead for 2.4 km (1½ miles) to Eden taking the B149 to the left towards Glenoe and Larne. The reservoir is on the left after 2.8 km (1¾ miles).

Lough Mourne: Take the B58 at Carrickfergus towards Ballynure for 2.4 km (1½ miles) to the first crossroads; turn right onto the B90 for 1.6 km (1 mile) to the next crossroads, turning left proceed for 2.4 km (1½ miles) to the next crossroads then turn right. The reservoir is 0.8 km (½ mile) along this road and on the left.

COUNTY ANTRIM

Craigavon City Park Lakes

Upper Bann River (Portadown)

(Designated coarse fishery)

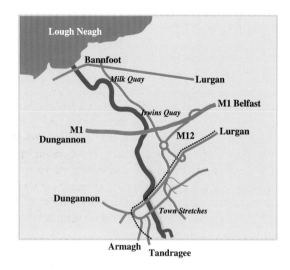

Nearest Town	- Portadown
Length	- 16 km (10 miles)
Species	- Pike, perch, roach, bream and trout
Season	- All year round for coarse fish - 1 March–31 October for trout
Methods	- All lawful methods, including ground bait and maggots for coarse fish
Bag Limit	- 2 pike per day
Size Limit	- Pike of 4 kg (8.8 lb) and over must be returned to the water
Other Restrictions	- Fishing on Sunday is not permitted on the Hoy's Meadow Stretch
Boats	- Fishing from boats is not permitted
Licence	- *Over 18* - Fisheries Conservancy Board Coarse Fishing Rod Licence (for coarse fish only) - *Under 18* - None
Permit	- *Over 18* - Department of Agriculture Coarse Fishing Permit (for coarse fish only) - *Under 18* - None.

Angling on the Upper Bann at Portadown

This stretch of the River Bann extends from Point of Whitecoat to Lough Neagh. It is one of the best known coarse fisheries in Europe, with the reaches in the Portadown town area established as big match venues.

The Department has provided an attractive path along the boulevard on the west bank from Point of Whitecoat to the boathouse. Craigavon Borough Council has provided a footpath from the boathouse through Shillington's Stretch, which they have developed mainly for pleasure anglers. Other stretches are frequently used for competitions. The Council has also developed an amenity area and constructed a number of fishing stands, including some for use by disabled anglers in the Council Stretch of Hoy's Meadow. Much of the east bank downstream of Portadown is also accessible.

Anglers should remember that the river is used for water sports, such as boating and canoeing, and courtesy should be exercised at all times. Five fishing areas have been developed by arrangement with the landowners involved. Access to other points may be obtained by anglers through private arrangement.

COUNTY ARMAGH

Upper Bann River

Anglers should be careful not to approach the river at points other than those listed, except with the permission of the landowners.

How to get there

Access to town areas:

Boulevard – from Craigavon via the A3 into Bridge Street crossing the Bann Bridge, take first left in Bridge Street South and continue about 275 metres (300 yards) to car-park on left. There is also access by foot via the path to the boathouse at the end of Portmore Street.

Hoy's Meadow – Going out of Portadown via Bridge Street towards Craigavon (the A3) crossing the Bann Bridge, take the second street on the left, Watson Street. Access to the amenity area and car-parks is via the tunnel under the flyover.

Portadown Park (opposite Hoy's Meadow) – going out of Portadown by Bridge Street and the A4 towards Dungannon under the flyover and passing the factory on the right take the second street on the right, Woodside Green, leading to open ground and playing fields by the river. There is a car-park area in Churchill Park reached via Woodside Green.

Country areas:

There are two access points to the river on the east bank. Both are off the B2 and signposted "Lough Neagh", which is best approached off the A27 to Craigavon.

– Irwin's Quay off the B2 on the left about 180 metres (200 yards) past the flyover across the M1 motorway.

– Milk Quay off the B2 by a lane to the left 4 km (2½ miles) past the flyover across the M1 motorway directly opposite Bailiff's Road.

ENVIRONMENT SERVICE

Department of
the Environment
for Northern Ireland

The Wildlife (NI) Order 1985 came into effect on April 15th 1985 and affords protection to many previously unprotected species of animals and plants.

Apart from a small number of 'pest' species, all birds are protected, including herons and cormorants.

The otter is also now fully protected.

Any fishing or angling organisation which experiences problems with any protected species should immediately contact Environment Service, Countryside and Wildlife on Belfast (0232) 230560 for advice.

A guide to the law on wildlife, entitled 'The Wildlife Law and You' is available from Environment Service, Countryside and Wildlife, Calvert House, 23 Castle Place, Belfast BT1 1FY.

PLEASE DO NOT DISCARD OLD FISHING TACKLE SUCH AS LINES, HOOKS OR LEAD WEIGHTS IN THE COUNTRYSIDE — TAKE THEM AWAY FOR DISPOSAL

RIVER BLACKWATER

(Including stretch designated as a coarse fishery)

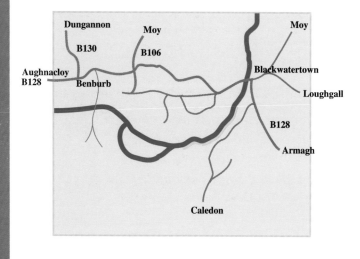

Nearest Town	- Blackwatertown
Length	- 2.5 km (1½ miles)
Species	- Salmon, brown trout (dollaghan in season), pike, perch, roach, bream and eels
Season	- 1 March–31 October for game fish All year for coarse fish downstream of Blackwatertown Bridge
Methods	- All lawful methods including ground bait and maggots for coarse fish
Bag Limit	- 2 pike per day
Size Limit	- Pike of 4 kg (8.8 lb) and over must be returned to the water
Other Restrictions	- None
Boats	- Fishing from boats is not permitted
Licence	- *Over 18* - Fisheries Conservancy Board Game Fishing Rod Licence is required, except for coarse fishing downstream of Blackwatertown Bridge, where a Coarse Fishing Rod Licence will be sufficient unless fishing specifically for salmon or trout

Permit	- ***Under 18*** - None
	- ***Over 18*** - Department of Agriculture Game Fishing Permit to fish upstream of Blackwatertown Bridge. If fishing for coarse fish only downstream of Blackwatertown Bridge, a Coarse Fishing Permit will suffice
	- ***Under 18*** - Department of Agriculture Juvenile Game Fishing Permit if fishing for salmon or trout.

This stretch of the River Blackwater, which lies mainly upstream of Blackwatertown Bridge, is available to Department permit holders on the right (Co Armagh) bank. Coarse fish abound in the lower part of this reach but there is a short stretch of good game fishing water downstream of the island where there are a number of known salmon lies.

Game fish stocks are now recovering following a drainage scheme in the late 1980s and restoration of the system.

HOW TO GET THERE

From Belfast by M1 motorway junction 15, take the A29 through Moy towards Armagh turning left towards Blackwatertown (signposted) at the edge of Charlemont village.

From Armagh take the A29 towards Moy, turning left onto the B128 at at McCready's Corner, 4.8 km (3 miles) from Armagh.

COUNTY ARMAGH

CLAY LAKE

(Designated coarse fishery)

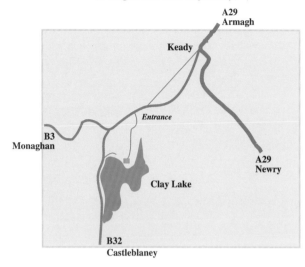

Nearest Town	- Keady
Area	- 48.6 hectares (120 acres)
Species	- Pike, rudd and perch
Season	- All year
Methods	- All lawful methods, but ground bait and maggots are not permitted
Bag Limit	- 2 pike per day
Size Limit	- Pike of 4 kg (8.8 lb) and over must be returned to the water
Other Restrictions	- None
Boats	- Fishing from boats is not permitted
Licence	- *Over 18* - Fisheries Conservancy Board Coarse Fishing Rod Licence
	- *Under 18* - None
Permit	- *Over 18* - Department of Agriculture Coarse Fishing Permit
	- *Under 18* - None.

Note: This is a public reservoir and care should be taken not to cause pollution.

Clay Lake, lying alongside the Castleblaney Road, is known for its large perch and heavy pike. The occasional trout is also caught.

Stiles and footsticks have been provided to give easy access along the shore, much of which is stony and safe for wading, although care should be taken in soft areas.

HOW TO GET THERE

From Armagh – south by A29 to Keady 13 km (8 miles), continuing towards Castleblaney on the B3 for 2 km (1¼ miles). The lake is on the left.

From Newry – north by A25 to Newtownhamilton, continuing on the A29 to Keady and turn left onto the B3 for 2 km (1¼ miles). The lake is on the left.

COUNTY ARMAGH

CRAIGAVON CITY PARK LAKES

North Lake - Designated coarse fishery
South Lake - Rainbow trout fishery

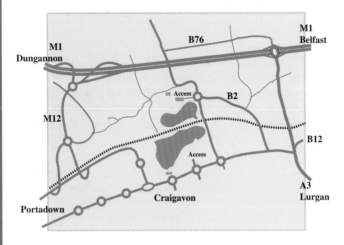

NORTH LAKE

Nearest Town	- Craigavon
Area	- 28.3 hectares (70 acres)
Species	- Pike, perch, roach and bream hybrids
Season	- All year
Methods	- All lawful methods
Bag Limit	- 2 pike per day
Size Limit	- Pike of 4 kg (8.8 lb) and over must be returned to the water
Other Restrictions	- Game fish must be returned to the water unless you have a game fishing permit and licence
Boats	- Fishing from non-mechanical boats is permitted
Licence	- *Over 18* - Fisheries Conservancy Board Coarse Fishing Rod Licence
	- *Under 18* - None
Permit	- *Over 18* - Department of Agriculture Coarse Fishing Permit
	- *Under 18* - None.

CRAIGAVON CITY PARK LAKES

SOUTH LAKE

Nearest Town	- Craigavon
Area	- 39.6 hectares (98 acres)
Species	- Rainbow trout
Season	- 1 February–31 December
Methods	- Fly fishing, spinning and worm fishing
Bag Limit	- 4 fish per rod per day
Size Limit	- Minimum takeable size 25.4 cm (10 inches)
Other Restrictions	- None
Boats	- Fishing from non-mechanical boats is permitted
Licence	- *Over 18* - Fisheries Conservancy Board Game Fishing Rod Licence
	- *Under 18* - None
Permit	- *Over 18* - Department of Agriculture Game Fishing Permit
	- *Under 18* - Department of Agriculture Juvenile Game Fishing Permit.

These lakes have been created primarily as a balancing reservoir to retain the run-off from the urban area and allow a controlled outflow to the Closet River.

Situated almost geographically central in the Craigavon designated area, they have been designed as a feature of the 332 hectare (820 acre) city park with provisions for boating and other forms of water recreation. Anglers may take their own boats. Boats are available for hire from Craigavon Borough Council Recreational Department.

South Lake is designated as a rainbow trout fishery and is stocked regularly from Movanagher Fish Farm.

HOW TO GET THERE

From Belfast by the M1 to the A76 spur to Lurgan, Craigavon. Turn towards Lurgan for 0.8 km (½ mile) and take a right turn by the A3 for 1.2 km (¾ mile) to the Tannaghmore Gardens roundabout to the North Lake. For the South Lake, take the road from the Tannaghmore Gardens roundabout to Portadown and turn off at roundabout No.3 on the Lurgan-Portadown road to the car-park.

Castlewellan Lake

BALLYKEEL LOUGHERNE

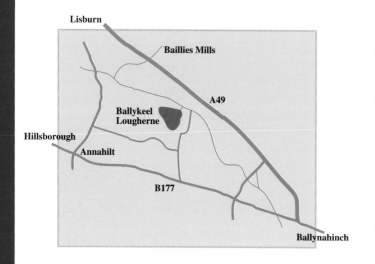

Nearest Town	- Ballynahinch
Area	- 21.4 hectares (53 acres)
Species	- Brown and rainbow trout
Season	- 1 March–31 October
Methods	- Fly fishing
Bag Limit	- 4 fish per rod per day
Size Limit	- Minimum takeable size 25.4 cm (10 inches)
Other Restrictions	- None
Boats	- Fishing from boats is not permitted
Licence	- *Over 18* - Fisheries Conservancy Board Game Fishing Rod Licence
	- *Under 18* - None
Permit	- *Over 18* - Department of Agriculture Game Fishing Permit
	- *Under 18* - Department of Agriculture Juvenile Game Fishing Permit.

This attractive lough is stocked regularly from Movanagher Fish Farm.

On the south side, the bank shelves steeply and wading should not be attempted. Fishing stands have been erected on the west side. An anglers' path is provided and anglers must use the only official entrance which is off the old Lisburn-Ballynahinch Road. Motorists should take care not to obstruct the road at this point or block farm entrances.

HOW TO GET THERE

From Ballynahinch take the A49 and B177 towards Hillsborough branching right 2 km (1¼ miles) out at the staggered crossroads. The entrance is 3.6 km (2¼ miles) on the left.

From Belfast take the M1. Turn off at the Lisburn/Saintfield intersection. Take the A49 towards Ballynahinch for 6.8 km (4¼ miles) to Baillies Mills. Turn left at the crossroads and right at the T-junction at the end of the road. The entrance is 2.4 km (1½ miles) on the right.

Hooked!

LOUGH BRICKLAND

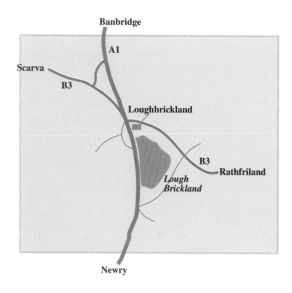

Nearest Town	- Banbridge
Area	- 25 hectares (62 acres)
Species	- Brown and rainbow trout
Season	- 1 March–31 October
Methods	- Fly fishing
Bag Limit	- 4 fish per rod per day
Size Limit	- Minimum takeable size 25.4 cm (10 inches)
Other Restrictions	- None
Boats	- Fishing from boats is not permitted
Licence	- *Over 18* - Fisheries Conservancy Board Game Fishing Rod Licence - *Under 18* - None
Permit	- *Over 18* - Department of Agriculture Game Fishing Permit - *Under 18* - Department of Agriculture Juvenile Game Fishing Permit.

Lough Brickland, alongside the main Belfast-Dublin Road, is stocked with both brown and rainbow trout from Movanagher Fish Farm.

The shore is mostly firm and safe for wading but the north and south tips should be avoided. A surfaced path is provided along the west shore with stiles and footsticks right around the lake, except at the south tip.

HOW TO GET THERE

From Belfast – M1 to Lisburn (Sprucefield roundabout) then the A1 towards Newry for 45 km (28 miles). The lough is on the left.

From Armagh – Take the A51 to Tandragee, the A27 to Scarva and B3 to Loughbrickland, joining the A1 in Loughbrickland village.

From Lurgan – Take the A26 to Banbridge and head south towards Newry by the A1.

From Newry – North by the A1 towards Banbridge for 16 km (10 miles).

FISHERMEN – CAST WITH CARE

LOOK OUT FOR OVERHEAD POWER LINES

YOUR CARBON FIBRE ROD IS AN EXCELLENT CONDUCTOR OF ELECTRICITY

COUNTY DOWN

CASTLEWELLAN LAKE

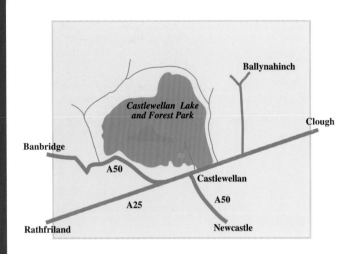

Note: Anglers using the forest car-park at Castlewellan have to pay the current forest car-park charges. There is a separate fee payable for launching a fishing boat.

Nearest Town - Castlewellan
Area - 41.6 hectares (103 acres)
Species - Brown and rainbow trout
Season - 1 March–31 October
Methods - Fly fishing, spinning and worm fishing
Fly fishing only from boats
Bag Limit - 4 fish per rod per day
Size Limit - Minimum takeable size 25.4 cm (10 inches)
Other Restrictions- None
Boats - Fishing from non-mechanical boats only, 8 am to dusk (maximum 10 boats at any one time; maximum 2 anglers per boat; no advance booking)
Note: Boats are not available for hire at the lake
Licence - *Over 18* - Fisheries Conservancy Board Game Fishing Rod Licence
- *Under 18* - None
Permit - *Over 18* - Department of Agriculture Game Fishing Permit
- *Under 18* - Department of Agriculture Juvenile Game Fishing Permit.

This is a very popular fishery. It is stocked regularly with brown and rainbow trout from Movanagher Fish Farm.

The lake is one of the main attractions of Castlewellan Forest Park. Other facilities include a car-park, cafeteria, caravan, camping and barbecue facilities. There are also scenic walks of varying lengths and it is possible to visit the arboretum and the Annesley garden, where greenhouses are open to the public.

A car-park for disabled anglers has been constructed near the lake.

The Department intends to promote greater use of the lake for water-based recreation, including canoeing, sailing and rowing. Consequently, it may be necessary to restrict the areas available for fishing and the days on which fishing from boats is permitted.

HOW TO GET THERE

Castlewellan lies on the main Downpatrick to Newry road (A25). The entrance to the forest park is signposted in the town.

From Newcastle, take the A50 northwards.

From Banbridge, take the A50 in a south-easterly direction.

COUNTY DOWN

LOUGH COWEY

(Managed by Ards District Fly Fishing Club)

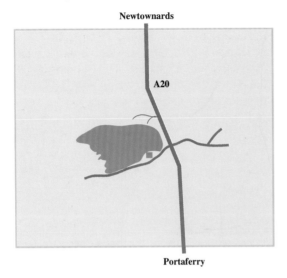

Nearest Town	- Portaferry
Area	- 18.2 hectares (45 acres)
Species	- Rainbow trout
Season	- All year
Methods	- Fly fishing
Bag Limit	- 1 fish (Department of Agriculture Permit holders) *(see notes)*
Size Limit	- None
Other Restrictions	- None
Boats	- Fishing permitted from non-mechanical boats which must be hired from the Club. Privately owned boats are not permitted
Licence	- *Over 18* - Fisheries Conservancy Board Game Fishing Rod Licence
	- *Under 18* - None
Day ticket	- *Over 18* - Ards District Fly Fishing Club Day Ticket
	- *Under 18* - Ards District Fly Fishing Club Day Ticket

Note: This is a public reservoir and care should be taken not to cause pollution.

Notes:

Under an agreement with the Department, Ards District Fly Fishing Club exercises the fishing rights on Lough Cowey. Ten day tickets are available daily, free of charge, to holders of Department of Agriculture Adult or Juvenile Game Season Permits. These may be obtained from the fishery office on site telephone: Portaferry (02477) 28946. Department permit holders fishing on a day ticket are permitted to retain one fish free of charge. Thereafter, if they wish to remain on the fishery, they must pay the appropriate day ticket charge. Other anglers may also purchase day tickets.

The southern shore and part of the lough is a bird sanctuary controlled by the National Trust and fishing is not allowed in this area.

A car-park and slipway are provided on the south shore. The ferry linking Strangford and Portaferry makes Lough Cowey easily accessible from Downpatrick and the lough is only 40 km (25 miles) from Belfast.

HOW TO GET THERE

From Belfast travel eastwards on the A20 to Newtownards. Continue on the A20 through Greyabbey and Kircubbin. The lough is on the right near the main road, 4 km (2½ miles) before you reach Portaferry.

COUNTY DOWN

HILLSBOROUGH LAKE

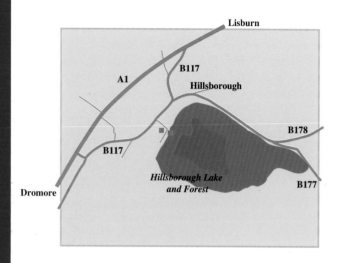

Nearest Town	- Hillsborough
Area	- 16.2 hectares (40 acres)
Species	- Rainbow trout
Season	- 1 February–31 December
Methods	- Fly fishing, spinning and worm fishing
Bag Limit	- 4 fish per rod per day
Size Limit	- Minimum takeable size 25.4 cm (10 inches)
Other Restrictions	- Fly fishing is not permitted from the dam or the shore adjacent to the dam nor in the vicinity of the footbridge at the southern point of the lake. These prohibited areas are signposted
Boats	- Fishing from boats is not permitted
Licence	- *Over 18* - Fisheries Conservancy Board Game Fishing Rod Licence - *Under 18* - None
Permit	- *Over 18* - Department of Agriculture Game Fishing Permit - *Under 18* - Department of Agriculture Juvenile Game Fishing Permit.

The lake is situated in Hillsborough Forest, a large park with scenic wooded parkland, forest walks and lakeside paths. It is a very popular centre for family picnics and walks, and in addition to the restrictions on fly fishing noted above, great care must be taken by anglers not to endanger the many pedestrians using the area. The lake is also a sanctuary for a great variety of wildlife, including swans and several varieties of ducks, whose interests must be preserved at all costs. Litter, lines and hooks must not be discarded.

Cars are not permitted beyond the forest park car-parks. Anglers must observe the closing times of the forest park which are displayed on the gates.

HOW TO GET THERE

From Belfast take the M1 to the Lisburn (Sprucefield) intersection. Take the A1 to Hillsborough, turning left just before the roundabout onto the B177 to go through the town. The entrance is signposted on the Dromore road as you leave the town.

From Ballynahinch, take the B177 to Hillsborough and go through the town, as above.

RIVER LAGAN

(Stretches controlled by Iveagh Angling Club)

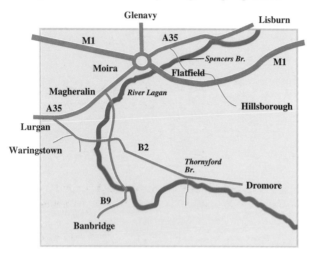

Nearest Towns	- Dromore, Magheralin, Moira, Lurgan
Length	- Approximately 11.27 km (7 miles)
Species	- Brown trout
Season	- 1 March–30 September
Methods	- Fly fishing only, except on the stretch of the river from the downstream side of Steps Bridge, Magheralin (near Express Dairy (NI) Ltd) to Spencer's Bridge, where from 1 June fly fishing, spinning and worm fishing are permitted
Bag Limit	- 6 fish per rod per day
Size Limit	- Minimum takeable size 25.4 cm (10 inches)
Other Restrictions	- Sunday fishing is not permitted except on the stretch between Steps Bridge and Spencer's Bridge (notices posted)
Boats	- Fishing from boats is not permitted
Licence	- *Over 18* - Fisheries Conservancy Board Game Fishing Rod Licence - *Under 18* - None

Day ticket   - *Over 18* - Iveagh Angling Club Day Ticket
- *Under 18* - Iveagh Angling Club Day Ticket *(see below)*

Under an agreement with the Department, Iveagh Angling Club exercises the fishing rights on all stretches of the River Lagan between Thornyford Bridge, outside Dromore, to Spencer's Bridge, Flatfield. Notices are posted at access points on all stretches indicating permitted methods, restrictions on Sunday fishing etc.

DAY TICKETS

Iveagh Angling Club makes an unlimited number of day tickets available to non-Club members. These day tickets are on sale at:-

Premier Angling, 17 Queen Street, Lurgan
McCarten's Bar, Donaghcloney
FC Computers and Tackle, 28 High Street, Lurgan.

In addition, ten daily tickets are available per day free of charge to holders of Department Annual Game

Season Permits on production of their adult or juvenile permits. These Club Day Tickets must be endorsed with the Department Permit Number and are available only from Sidney Beckett, 54 High Street, Lurgan (telephone: (0762) 23352).

Note: Club Day Tickets issued for Sunday fishing do *not* permit holders to fish those areas signposted "No Sunday Fishing".

HOW TO GET THERE

Dromore is just off the A1 between Lisburn and Banbridge, where it meets the B2 from Ballynahinch.

Magheralin is on the A3 Moira to Lurgan road where it meets the B9 from Donaghcloney and Banbridge.

Moira is at junction 9 of the M1.

Lurgan can be approached by leaving the M1 either at junction 9 and taking the A3 through Moira, or at junction 10 and following the signposts for the town centre.

COUNTY DOWN

LOUGH MONEY

(Designated coarse fishery)

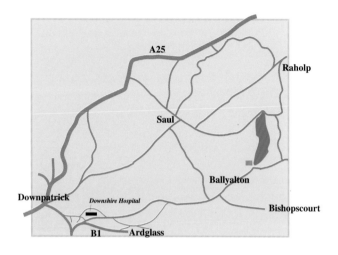

Nearest Town	- Downpatrick
Area	- 21.4 hectares (53 acres)
Species	- Pike, perch and eels
Season	- All year
Methods	- All lawful methods but ground bait and maggots are not permitted
Bag Limit	- 2 pike per day
Size Limit	- Pike of 4 kg (8.8 lb) and over must be returned to the water
Other Restrictions	- None
Boats	- Fishing from boats is not permitted
Licence	- *Over 18* - Fisheries Conservancy Board Coarse Fishing Rod Licence
	- *Under 18* - None
Permit	- *Over 18* - Department of Agriculture Coarse Fishing Permit
	- *Under 18* - None

Note: This is a public reservoir and care should be taken not to cause pollution.

Lough Money lies hidden away in rocky countryside near Ballyalton, 4 km (2½ miles) directly east of Downpatrick. The shores are almost all rocky and firm for wading, but fishing is not allowed in the fenced-off area at the pump house. The water is deeper and there is less weed growth near the east bank.

HOW TO GET THERE

From Downpatrick take the B1 towards Ardglass, keeping left at the Downshire Hospital just outside the town towards Ballyalton and Ballyhornan as far as Ballyalton. Just past Ballyalton, fork left off the Ballyhornan Road for 0.8 km (½ mile) to the lough.

Motorists are asked to use the car-park provided and not to block the roads in the area.

Lough Money

COUNTY DOWN

PORTAVOE RESERVOIR

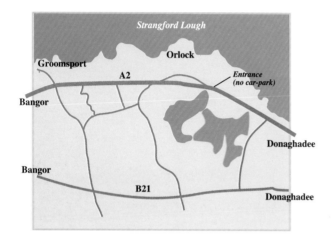

Nearest Towns	- Donaghadee, Bangor
Area	- 12.5 hectares (31 acres)
Species	- Brown and rainbow trout
Season	- 1 March–31 October
Methods	- Fly fishing only
Bag Limit	- 4 fish per rod per day
Size Limit	- Minimum takeable size 25.4 cm (10 inches)
Other Restrictions	- Only 20 rods allowed at any one time
Boats	- Fishing from boats is not permitted
Licence	- *Over 18* - Fisheries Conservancy Board Game Fishing Rod Licence - *Under 18* - None
Permit	- *Over 18* - Department of Agriculture Game Fishing Permit - *Under 18* - Department of Agriculture Juvenile Game Fishing Permit.

Note: This is a public reservoir and care must be taken not to cause pollution.

This small and very attractive reservoir lies on the coast road between Donaghadee and Bangor. With the increasing demands on all public reservoirs, the water level tends to drop considerably in the summer.

Regular stocking from Movanagher Fish Farm ensures good fishing on this popular fishery.

HOW TO GET THERE

From Belfast by the A2 via Holywood towards Bangor. Join Bangor Ring Road turning right towards Donaghadee. Continue on the Ring Road as far as the Groomsport roundabout (fifth and last roundabout). Turn right towards Donaghadee on the A2. The reservoir is about 4 km (2½ miles) along this road. Cars may be parked on the hard shoulder of the A2, but are not allowed into the waterworks grounds. The entrance to the reservoir must not be blocked.

Portavoe Reservoir

COUNTY DOWN

QUOILE BASIN AND RIVER

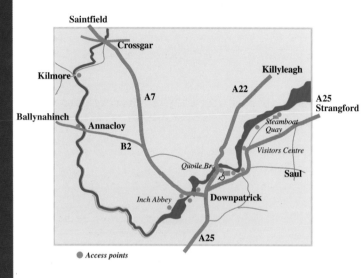

● *Access points*

Nearest Town	- Downpatrick
Area	- 40 hectares (100 acres) in basin, and 11.25 km (7 miles) of river
Species	- Pike, perch, rudd, eels and brown trout
Season	- All year for coarse fishing, 1 March–31 October for trout
Methods	- Fly fishing, spinning and worm fishing for trout. All lawful methods including ground bait and maggots for coarse fish. Digging for bait is prohibited
Bag Limit	- 2 pike per day
Size Limit	- Pike of 4 kg (8.8 lb) and over must be returned to the water
Other Restrictions	- Fishing is permitted as far as Steamboat Quay, from the south bank only. No fishing is permitted downstream of Steamboat Quay in the interests of the National Nature Reserve. No wading permitted
Boats	- Fishing from boats is not permitted

Licence	- *Over 18* - Fisheries Conservancy Board Coarse Fishing Rod Licence (for coarse fish only) Fisheries Conservancy Board Game Fishing Rod Licence if fishing for trout
	- *Under 18* - None
Permit	- *Over 18* - Department of Agriculture Coarse Fishing Permit (for coarse fish only) Department of Agriculture Game Fishing Permit if fishing for trout
	- *Under 18* - Department of Agriculture Juvenile Game Fishing Permit if fishing for trout.

The fishing rights of the basin from the old barrier (flood gates) at Quoile Bridge to the new barrier at the head of Strangford Lough are owned by the Department of Agriculture. Access to the water is easy on the south side where the road runs near the water. A path and some stands have been provided and a disabled anglers' car-park is now available at the old flood gates. Application for keys to the Quoile Countryside Centre, 5 Quay Road, Downpatrick, telephone: (0396) 615520.

This is a National Nature Reserve, managed by the Environment Service of the Department of the Environment, and anglers are requested to be careful to cause as little disturbance as possible to wildlife and to take care not to leave pieces of line, lead shot or other litter.

The Department of Agriculture also leases the fishing rights of the river from Downpatrick to Kilmore.

Access points are marked on the map.

HOW TO GET THERE

From Belfast, proceed in a southerly direction by the A24 and A7 through Saintfield to Downpatrick.

Kilmore is on the minor road which runs due south out of Crossgar.

Annacloy is on the B2 which forks left off the A7, 2.4 km (1½ miles) from Downpatrick.

COUNTY DOWN

SHIMNA RIVER
(TOLLYMORE FOREST PARK)

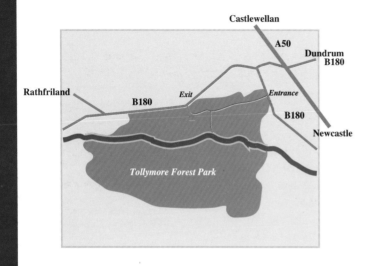

Nearest Town	- Newcastle
Length	- 4 km (2½ miles), (stretch within Tollymore Forest Park only)
Species	- Sea trout and salmon in season
Season	- 1 March–31 October
Methods	- Fly fishing, spinning and worm fishing
Bag Limit	- 2 salmon or sea trout per rod per day
Size Limit	- None
Other Restrictions	- Fishing on Sunday not permitted. Anglers must cease fishing when the bag limit is taken
Boats	- Fishing from boats is not permitted
Licence	- *Over 18* - Fisheries Conservancy Board Game Fishing Rod Licence - *Under 18* - None

Note: Car-park – Anglers using the forest car-park at Tollymore are liable for the current forest car-park charges.
Pedestrians – There is a pedestrian charge at the Bryansford gate entrance.

Permit	- *Over 18* - Department of Agriculture Game Fishing Permit
	- *Under 18* - Department of Agriculture Juvenile Game Fishing Permit
Day tickets	- Day tickets, limited to 6 per day, are also required between 1 August and 31 October. These may be booked at Tollymore Forest Office (see below).

This stretch of the Shimna, which is situated in Ulster's premier forest park, has been owned by the Department since 1 July 1975. From August onwards salmon appear. The clear water and rocky pools call for special techniques but the skilled angler has a good chance of getting his bag limit when the fish are running.

Permits are available from the Forest Office at Tollymore Forest Park Monday–Friday 8 am–4.30 pm. Phone Newcastle (03967) 22428. Outside office hours permits are available from the Forest Ranger. Reserved booking must be paid for in advance. Each angler will be allowed to hold only one special permit at any time.

The holder must exercise his privilege in a sportsmanlike manner and not interfere with other permit holders.

Anglers should note that Department permits are valid only inside the limits of the Department's stretch (Forestry Area).

Tollymore Forest Park was the first of Northern Ireland's forests to be designated as a forest park. It offers facilities for caravans and camping. Recreational facilities include a visitor centre, cafe, toilets, arboretum and waymarked trails. Horse-riding is also permitted.

HOW TO GET THERE

Newcastle is on the A2 from Belfast. The forest park is signposted.

SPELGA RESERVOIR

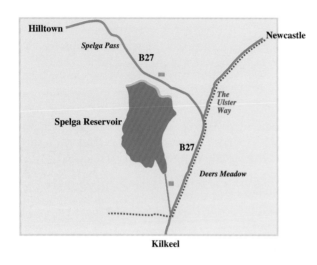

Nearest Town	- Hilltown
Area	- 60 hectares (148 acres)
Species	- Brown trout
Season	- 1 March–31 October
Methods	- Fly fishing, spinning and worm fishing
Bag Limit	- None
Size Limit	- None
Other Restrictions	- None
Boats	- Fishing from boats is not permitted
Licence	- *Over 18* - Fisheries Conservancy Board Game Fishing Rod Licence
	- *Under 18* - None
Permit	- *Over 18* - Department of Agriculture Game Fishing Permit
	- *Under 18* - Department of Agriculture Juvenile Game Fishing Permit.

Note: This is a public reservoir and care should be taken not to cause pollution.

This reservoir, set in rugged surroundings in the heart of the Mournes near the source of the River Bann, supplies water to the Portadown and Banbridge areas. Opened for angling to Department permit holders for the first time in 1971, it has proved popular – particularly during the summer months.

HOW TO GET THERE

From Rathfriland, south on the B25 to Hilltown, then take the B8 and B27 towards Newcastle, forking right after 2.4 km (1½ miles) towards Kilkeel for 4 km (2½ miles) until reaching Spelga at the head of the valley (signposted).

From Newry by the A25 and B8 to Hilltown.

From Belfast by the A24 through Ballynahinch to Clough, turning right onto the A25 through Castlewellan and 8 km (5 miles) beyond this, fork left for Hilltown (B8) turning left for Kilkeel (B27) before entering the town.

Spelga Reservoir

COUNTY DOWN

91

Lower Lough Erne

BALLINAMALLARD RIVER (RIVERSDALE)

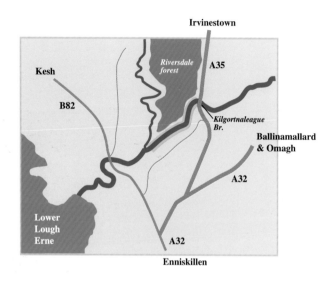

Nearest Town	- Ballinamallard
Length	- 1.6 km (1 mile)
Species	- Brown trout and salmon
Season	- 1 March–30 September
Methods	- Fly fishing, spinning and worm fishing
Bag Limit	- 4 fish per rod per day
Size Limit	- Minimum takeable size 25.4 cm (10 inches)
Other Restrictions	- None
Boats	- Fishing from boats is not permitted
Licence	- *Over 18* - Fisheries Conservancy Board Game Fishing Rod Licence - *Under 18* - None
Permit	- *Over 18* - Department of Agriculture Game Fishing Permit - *Under 18* - Department of Agriculture Juvenile Game Fishing Permit.

BALLINAMALLARD RIVER (RIVERSDALE)

This is a small but highly productive river with trout as the main species. There are also some salmon from mid-July in suitable conditions.

The Riversdale Stretch is a very attractive angling water situated in pleasant woodland.

HOW TO GET THERE

The entrance is off the A35 Enniskillen to Irvinestown road at Kilgortnaleague Bridge.

Ballinamallard River

95

COLEBROOK RIVER

(Designated coarse fishery)

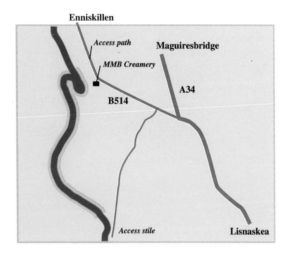

Nearest Town	- Lisnaskea
Length	- 3.2 km (2 miles)
Species	- Roach, bream, perch, rudd, eels and the occasional pike, trout and salmon
Season	- All year for coarse fish. 1 March–30 September for trout and salmon
Methods	- Fly fishing, spinning and worm fishing for trout and salmon. All lawful methods including ground bait and maggots for coarse fish
Bag Limit	- 2 pike per day
Size Limit	- Pike of 4 kg (8.8 lb) and over must be returned to the water
Other Restrictions	- None
Boats	- Fishing from boats is not permitted

Licence	- *Over 18* - Fisheries Conservancy Board Coarse Fishing Rod Licence (for coarse fish only) Fisheries Conservancy Board Game Fishing Rod Licence if fishing for salmon or trout
	- *Under 18* - None
Permit	- *Over 18* - Department of Agriculture Coarse Fishing Permit (for coarse fish only). Department of Agriculture Game Fishing Permit if fishing for salmon or trout
	- *Under 18* - Department of Agriculture Juvenile Game Fishing Permit if fishing for salmon or trout.

This is an excellent coarse angling water. Large bream and roach are in abundance with perch and rudd also present. Salmon are scarce but big brown trout are often taken towards the end of the season.

HOW TO GET THERE

From Lisnaskea proceed for 0.8 km (½ mile) along the A34 towards Maguiresbridge, turn left and proceed along the B514 to the MMB Creamery, where there is access.

COUNTY FERMANAGH

UPPER AND LOWER LOUGH ERNE

(Including areas designated as coarse fisheries)

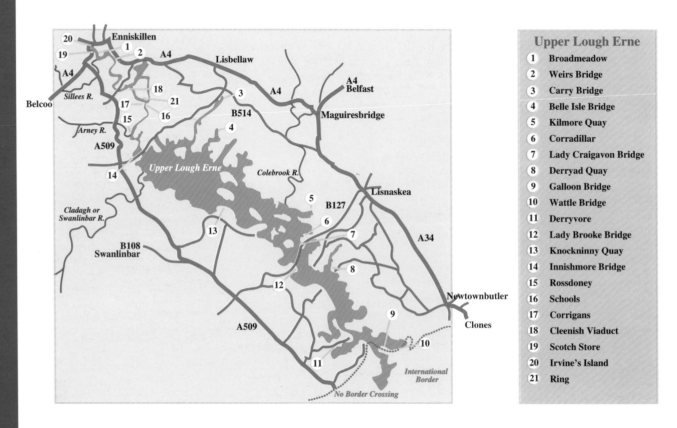

Upper Lough Erne

1. Broadmeadow
2. Weirs Bridge
3. Carry Bridge
4. Belle Isle Bridge
5. Kilmore Quay
6. Corradillar
7. Lady Craigavon Bridge
8. Derryad Quay
9. Galloon Bridge
10. Wattle Bridge
11. Derryvore
12. Lady Brooke Bridge
13. Knockninny Quay
14. Innishmore Bridge
15. Rossdoney
16. Schools
17. Corrigans
18. Cleenish Viaduct
19. Scotch Store
20. Irvine's Island
21. Ring

UPPER AND LOWER LOUGH ERNE

(Including areas designated as coarse fisheries)

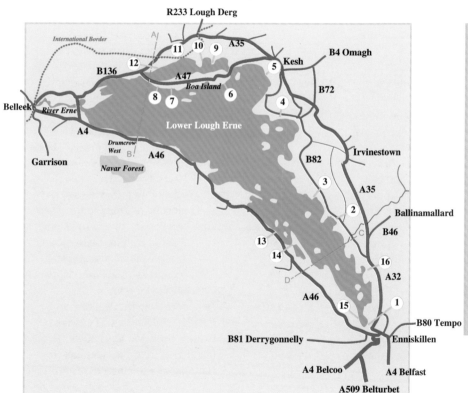

R233 Lough Derg
International Border
11 10 9   A35
12   B4 Omagh
B136   Kesh
A47   5
Boa Island B72
Belleek   8   7   6
River Erne   4
A4   Lower Lough Erne
Garrison   Drumcrow
            West   A46
            Navar Forest   B82   Irvinestown
                    3   A35
                    2   Ballinamallard
                            B46
            13   16
            14   A32
            A46   1
                    15   B80 Tempo
B81 Derrygonnelly   Enniskillen
        A4 Belcoo   A4 Belfast
            A509 Belturbet

Lower Lough Erne

1. Cornagrade
2. Goblusk Landing Stage
3. Rossigh (Picnic Area)
4. Castle Archdale Forest
5. Muckross
6. Boa Island (East End)
7. Acheson's Quay
8. Boa Island (West End) and Drennan
9. Clonelly
10. Curraghmore
11. Lowery
12. Sandy Bay
13. Blaney (Picnic Area)
14. Carrickreagh
15. Round 'O' Quay
16. Trory

COUNTY FERMANAGH

Upper and Lower Lough Erne

Principal Town - Enniskillen

Area - 15,303 hectares (37,800 acres)

Species - Brown trout, eel, pike, perch, rudd, bream, roach, salmon and sea trout

Season - 1 March–30 September for salmon, sea trout and brown trout
All year for coarse fish in designated coarse fishing areas

Methods - Fly fishing, spinning and worm fishing for trout, salmon and sea trout. All lawful methods including ground bait and maggots for coarse fish in Upper Lough Erne and in that portion of Lower Lough Erne east of an imaginary line running approximately south-west from the point where the A47 from Belleek to Boa Island leaves the mainland in the townland of Tawnawanny, touching the most westerly point of Binghams Rock and the most easterly part of Hills Island and on to where it hits the mainland in the townland of Drumcrow West (line A–B on Lower Lough Erne map).

When trolling, fishing rods and lines or hand lines shall not be used in excess of:-

(a) four in a boat occupied by three or more people

(b) three in a boat occupied by two people, and

(c) two in a boat occupied by one person

Bag Limit - *(Game Fishing)* 6 trout per rod per day
(Coarse Fishing) 2 pike per rod per day

Size Limit - Minimum takeable size for trout 30 cm (12 inches)
- Pike of 4 kg (8.8 lb) and over must be returned to the water

Other Restrictions - None

Boats - Fishing from mechanical and non-mechanical boats is permitted on both the Upper and Lower Loughs

Licence - *Over 18* - Fisheries Board Game Fishing Rod Licence is required if fishing north and west of an imaginary line drawn from the mouth of the Ballinamallard River on the northern shore to the nearest point of the shore opposite Castlehume on the eastern shore (line C–D on the Lower Lough Erne map). The only exception from the above is for fishing for coarse fish from the mainland, in which case the Coarse Fishing Rod Licence is sufficient. If fishing south and east of this line a Coarse Fishing Rod Licence will be sufficient unless fishing specifically for salmon or trout

- *Under 18* - None

Permit - *Over 18* - A similar division applies as for licences above, that is, Department of Agriculture Game Fishing Permit north of the line except for coarse fishing from shores; Coarse Fishing Permit south of the line. As in the case of licences, the Game Permit covers the whole of both Upper and Lower Loughs

- *Under 18* - Department of Agriculture Juvenile Game Fishing Permit if fishing for salmon or sea trout

Note – Unlike any of the other Department game fisheries, persons under 18 years of age do not require a permit when fishing on Lough Erne unless they are fishing for salmon or sea trout.

The most popular locations are indicated on the maps. At many of these, fishing stands have been erected to aid access to fishing.

GAME FISHING

Brown trout are the main quarry found almost exclusively in the Lower Lough, which is one of the best stocked lakes in Ireland due to natural recruitment plus the added benefit of annual artificial stocking by the Department. Anglers frequenting this internationally noted fishery can expect to capture trout well up into double figure weights.

From July onwards there may be some grilse fishing. It is likely that grilse runs will improve as the Department progresses a salmon enhancement programme.

101

Upper and Lower Lough Erne

Recommended areas for salmon fishing are from Rosscor Bridge up to Heron Island and across to the Garvary River.

Coarse fishing

Lough Erne is one of the finest coarse fishing waters in Europe and has become popular as a competition venue for British anglers. Roach are everywhere with bream, pike, perch and eels, in abundance. In recent years many outstanding weights were recorded during sponsored coarse angling competitions. These included two five-hour world match records. The Department continues to provide and maintain shore fixtures for the convenience of anglers. The Department's scientists have recently carried out an extensive coarse fish survey which indicates that fish are plentiful throughout this vast water.

Hire of boats

Boats can be hired at various locations, including the following:

- Manville House, Aughablaney, Letter (contact Mrs R A Graham)
- Carrybridge Angling Centre, Lisbellaw, telephone: (0365) 87651
- Lough Erne Hotel, Kesh, telephone: (03656) 31275
- Stella Marine, Castle Archdale
- Lakeland Marina Ltd, Muckross, Kesh, telephone: (03656) 31414
- Carlton Fishing Centre, Belleek, telephone: (03656) 58181
- Melvin Tackle, Main Street, Garrison (contact Sean Maguire, telephone: (0365) 658194).

How to get there

Enniskillen is the best starting place. There is a visitors centre and tourist information office just off the A4 in the town at the Lakeland Centre, telephone: (0365) 323110.

Lough Erne

RIVER ERNE (BELLEEK)

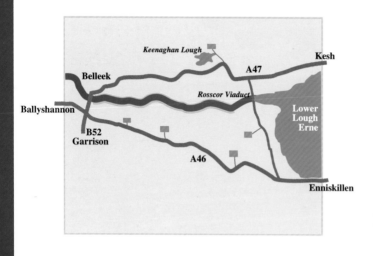

Nearest Town	- Belleek
Length	- 6 km (3¾ miles)
Species	- Brown trout and salmon
Season	- 1 March–30 September for trout and salmon
Methods	- Fly fishing, spinning and worm fishing Fly fishing only from boats
Bag Limit	- 6 trout per rod per day
Size Limit	- Minimum takeable size for trout 30 cm (12 inches)
Other Restrictions	- None
Boats	- Fishing is permitted from mechanical and non-mechanical boats
Licence	- *Over 18* - Fisheries Conservancy Board Game Fishing Rod Licence - *Under 18* - None
Permit	- *Over 18* - Department of Agriculture Game Fishing Permit - *Under 18* - Department of Agriculture Juvenile Game Fishing Permit.

The River Erne is notable as a game fishery. Large trout are present and are mainly taken during the late evenings or in the mayfly season, which lasts from mid-May to mid-June. Later in the season very good sedge fishing is available with trout up to 2.7 kg (6 lb) recorded.

BOAT HIRE

Carlton Fishing Centre, Belleek,
telephone: (03656) 58181.

There is ample car-parking at nearby Castle Caldwell Forest, with nature trails along the shore of Lough Erne and in the woodland, and a hide where wildfowl can be observed.

HOW TO GET THERE

From Enniskillen 30.5 km (19 miles) along the shore road (A46) adjacent to the edge of Lough Erne, or, via the B82 to Kesh and the A47 for 24 km (15 miles), turn left after Castle Caldwell onto the A46 to Rosscor viaduct.

ANGLING SAFETY TIPS

FISHING FROM A BOAT OR WADING?

WEAR A BUOYANCY AID OR BETTER STILL, A LIFE-JACKET

WHEN ANGLING – THINK SAFETY

COUNTY FERMANAGH

LOUGH KEENAGHAN

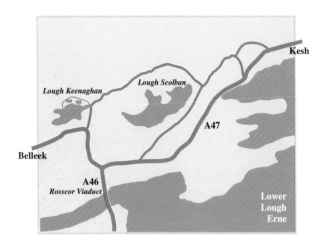

Nearest Town	- Belleek
Area	- 15.3 hectares (38 acres)
Species	- Brown trout
Season	- 1 March–31 October
Methods	- Fly fishing
Bag Limit	- 4 fish per rod per day
Size Limit	- Minimum takeable size 25.4 cm (10 inches)
Other Restrictions	- None
Boats	- Fishing is permitted from non-mechanical boats only
Licence	- *Over 18* - Fisheries Conservancy Board Game Fishing Rod Licence
	- *Under 18* - None
Permit	- *Over 18* - Department of Agriculture Game Fishing Permit
	- *Under 18* - Department of Agriculture Juvenile Game Fishing Permit.

LOUGH KEENAGHAN

Keenaghan is a very popular lake which attracts anglers from near and far. The north and south shores are mostly hard bottomed and easy to wade. Fishing from the western shore is impeded by bulrush and other aquatic weeds. Where shore angling is difficult, a number of wooden stands are provided. There is a car-park on the north side with a hardcore access road.

The lake provides unsurpassed brown trout angling and is regularly stocked with fish from Movanagher Fish Farm.

Boats may be hired from Sean Maguire, Melvin Tackle, Main Street, Garrison, telephone: (0365) 658194.

HOW TO GET THERE

Lough Keenaghan is approximately 2.4 km (1½ miles) from Belleek village and lies along the main Kesh to Belleek road (A47).

Lough Keenaghan

KILLYFOLE, CORRANNY AND CORRY

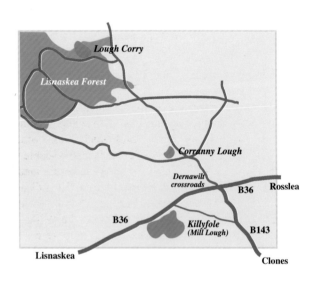

Nearest Town	- Rosslea
Areas	- Killyfole 22.6 hectares (56 acres)
	Corranny 4.6 hectares (11½ acres)
	Corry 6.5 hectares (16 acres)
Species	- Killyfole - pike and perch
	Corranny - brown and rainbow trout
	Corry - brown and rainbow trout
Season	- Killyfole - Open all year
	Corry and Corranny - 1 March– 31 October
Methods	- Fly fishing, spinning and worm fishing on Corry and Corranny. Fly fishing only from boats on Corry
	All lawful methods including ground bait or maggots on Killyfole
Bag Limit	- Killyfole - 2 pike per day
	- Corry and Corranny - 4 fish per rod per day

Size Limit	- Killyfole - Pike of 4 kg (8.8 lb) and over must be returned to the water
	- Corry and Corranny - Minimum takeable size 25.4 cm (10 inches)
Other Restrictions	- None
Boats	- Fishing is permitted from non-mechanical boats only on Corry
	Fishing from boats is not permitted on Killyfole and Corranny
Licence	- *Over 18* - Killyfole - Fisheries Conservancy Board Coarse Fishing Rod Licence.
	Corry and Corranny - Fisheries Conservancy Board Game Fishing Rod Licence
	- *Under 18* - None
Permit	- *Over 18* - Killyfole - Department of Agriculture Coarse Fishing Permit
	Corry and Corranny - Department of Agriculture Game Fishing Permit

- *Under 18* - Killyfole - None
Corry and Corranny - Department of Agriculture Juvenile Game Fishing Permit.

Killyfole (Mill Lough)

This is a waterworks reservoir between Lisnaskea and Rosslea in east Fermanagh. The south side is firm and gravelly with a long sloping shelf which is very good and safe for wading. The north side is also wadable but the going is softer and there is a very dangerous area in the north-west corner where a warning notice indicates sandy banks and deep water. Fishing is prohibited in the region of the treatment plant. During the 1970s pike became plentiful, and later when perch were introduced the water was managed as a mixed fishery. In more recent years trout stocking was discontinued and the lake reverted to coarse fish only. Killyfole is now a designated coarse fishery.

Corranny

Corranny is a small lough lying where the road forks near Dernawilt crossroads. There is a car-park, shore path and eleven fishing stands.

County Fermanagh

KILLYFOLE, CORRANNY AND CORRY

CORRY

This mountain lough in Lisnaskea Forest is noted for lively brown trout fishing. The shores are wadable on one side and a loughside car-park is provided.

HOW TO GET THERE

From Belfast to the M1 and A4 to Fivemiletown where you take the second road on the left towards Cooneen and Carnmore. Corry (signposted) lies on the right just before you reach the scenic area at Carnmore, 12 km (7½ miles) from Fivemiletown. Corranny is on the right 3.2 km (2 miles) further. For Killyfole (Mill Lough) go past Corranny about 1.6 km (1 mile) to Dernawilt crossroads turning right onto the B36. The lake is on the left after about 1.6 km (1 mile).

From Lisnaskea south-east by the A34 to Moorlough Cross turning left by the B36 towards Roslea. Killyfole is 6.4 km (4 miles) along the road on the right. For Corry and Corranny turn left at Dernawilt crossroads and go for 1.6 km (1 mile) for Corranny and 4.8 km (3 miles) for Corry.

Respect *the* life *of the* countryside

- Where stiles are provided – *use them*
- If you open a gate – *close it and secure it*
- If you climb over a gate – *do so at the hinged end*
- Stay on paths – *do not trample grass or other crops*
- Avoid contact with farm animals – *and in particular avoid land on which farm animals are grazing*
- Avoid damaging fences, hedges and walls
- Guard against risks of fire
- Keep dogs under control
- Leave no litter
- Safeguard water supplies
- Protect wildlife, plants and trees
- Go carefully on country roads

Lough Melvin

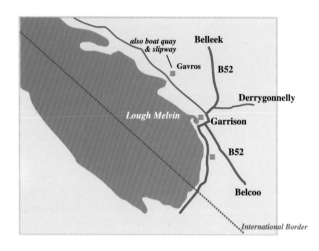

Nearest Town	- Garrison
Area	- 424 hectares (1,050 acres)
Species	- Spring salmon, grilse, brown trout (including sonaghan, gillaroo and ferox)
Season	- 1 February–30 September
Methods	- Fly fishing, spinning and worm fishing for trout from the shore and from boats. Fly fishing, spinning, worm fishing and trolling for salmon

When trolling, fishing rods and lines shall not be used in excess of:-

(a) four in a boat occupied by three or more people
(b) three in a boat occupied by two people, and
(c) two in a boat occupied by one person

Bag Limit	- None
Size Limit	- None
Other Restrictions	- None
Boats	- Fishing is permitted from both mechanical and non-mechanical boats

Licence — *Over 18* - Fisheries Conservancy Board Game Fishing Rod Licence
— *Under 18* - None

Permit — *Over 18* - Department of Agriculture Game Fishing Permit
— *Under 18* - Department of Agriculture Juvenile Game Fishing Permit.

(Note that Department permits are valid only in the Northern Ireland area of the lough – a separate permit is required for the Rossinver Fishery).

Lough Melvin is renowned for its salmon fishing and provides the only opportunity to catch salmon in Northern Ireland from the early spring run. The spring salmon which are caught range up to 9 kg (20 lb) with grilse averaging 2.25 kg (5 lb). The trout average 0.5 kg (1 lb) and include the interesting varieties of gillaroo, sonaghan and ferox.

The lough is situated at the extreme western end of County Fermanagh and straddles the border with the Republic of Ireland. The Northern Ireland portion of the water is centred on the town of Garrison with a shoreline of 5.6 km (3½ miles) extending from Blair's Bridge in the south-east to Inniskeen in the north, and an offshore projection in the region of 1 km (½ mile).

Three car-parks are provided, all with direct access to a shore path along the lough.

BOATS FOR HIRE:-

Carlton Fishing Centre, Belleek,
telephone: (03656) 58181
M Gilroy, Melvin Bar, Garrison,
telephone: (03656) 58380
Sean Maguire, Melvin Tackle, Main Street, Garrison,
telephone: (03656) 58194.

HOW TO GET THERE

From Enniskillen by the A4 to Belcoo, turning right by the B52 to Garrison. This route skirts the shores of the lovely Loughs Macnean and Lattone.

Alternatively, from Enniskillen by the A46 and B81 to Derrygonnelly. Turn left at the crossroads, 2.4 km (1½ miles) out of Derrygonnelly to go past the Lough Navar Forest entrance; 5.6 km (3½ miles) past the entrance fork left and then turn right at the next crossroads for Garrison.

MILL LOUGH (BELLANALECK)

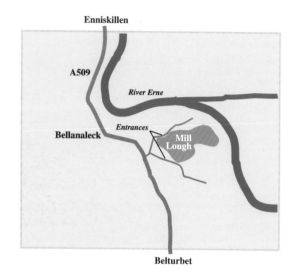

Nearest Town	- Enniskillen
Area	- 40 hectares (100 acres)
Species	- Rainbow and brown trout
Season	- 1 March–31 October
Methods	- Fly fishing only from boat and shore
Bag Limit	- 4 fish per rod per day
Size Limit	- Minimum takeable size 25.4 cm (10 inches)
Other Restrictions	- None
Boats	- Fishing is permitted from non-mechanical boats only which must be hired from the riparian owners listed. Privately owned boats are not permitted
Licence	- *Over 18* - Fisheries Conservancy Board Game Fishing Rod Licence
	- *Under 18* - None
Permit	- *Over 18* - Department of Agriculture Game Fishing Permit
	- *Under 18* - Department of Agriculture Juvenile Game Fishing Permit.

Since it was opened for angling, this fishery has offered excellent brown and rainbow trout fishing and has proved extremely popular.

There are two car-parks on the lough shore with a pathway along almost the full length of the northern shore. There are ten fishing stands situated where access is difficult. The shores are well indented and varied with large stretches of clean stony areas on the eastern and southern shores. Some patches of marl underlie the stones, causing some difficulty when wading.

BOATS FOR HIRE:-

G A Cathcart, Bellanaleck, telephone: (0365) 348232
J Foster, Toneyloman, Bellanaleck,
telephone: (0365) 348313
G L Stephenson, Tully, Bellanaleck

HOW TO GET THERE

Take the A4 through Enniskillen towards Belcoo to the junction with the A509, 3.2 km (2 miles) out of Enniskillen. Turn left for 4.8 km (3 miles), continue through Bellanaleck village and turn left on the outskirts at the side road to the lake (signposted).

Mill Lough

COUNTY FERMANAGH

115

Navar Forest Lakes – Achork, Glencreawan, Meenameen

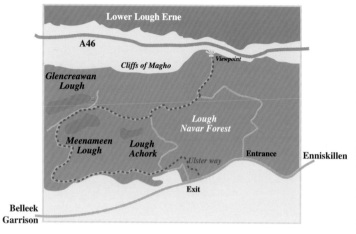

Nearest Town	- Derrygonnelly
Area	- Achork 4 hectares (10 acres) Glencreawan 19 hectares (47 acres) Meenameen 18.6 hectares (46 acres)
Species	- Brown and rainbow trout
Season	- 1 March–31 October
Methods	- Fly fishing, spinning and worm fishing Fly fishing only from boats
Bag Limit	- 4 fish per rod per day
Restrictions	- Minimum takeable size 25.4 cm (10 inches)
Boats	- Fishing is permitted from non-mechanical boats only
Licence	- *Over 18* - Fisheries Conservancy Board Game Fishing Rod Licence
	- *Under 18* - None
Permit	- *Over 18* - Department of Agriculture Game Fishing Permit
	- *Under 18* - Department of Agriculture Juvenile Game Fishing Permit

NAVAR FOREST LAKES - ACHORK, GLENCREAWAN, MEENAMEEN

Note – Anglers are liable for the normal charge for cars using the forest drive.

Navar Forest Park is administered by the Department's Forest Service.

Within the forest area there is a superb 11.2 km (7 mile) scenic drive, cliff-top viewpoint and a touring caravan site. There are three lakes open to Department permit holders – Achork, Glencreawan and Meenameen. Fishing is not permitted in the fourth lake (Lough Navar). Achork and Meenamen contain good stocks of brown trout. A car-park is provided at each lake.

These lakes are considered ideal for family outings as there is beautiful scenery, picnic areas and forest walks. Car-parks are at the water's edge at Glencreawan and Meenameen and alongside the adjacent forest road at Achork.

HOW TO GET THERE

From Enniskillen by A46 and B81 through Derrygonnelly 14.5 km (9 miles) following the forestry signposts (scenic drive).

From Belleek follow the forest drive signs from the village.

COUNTY FERMANAGH

LOUGH SCOLBAN

(Designated coarse fishery)

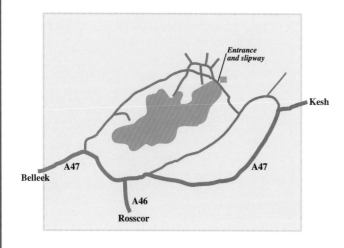

Nearest Town	- Belleek
Area	- 69 hectares (171 acres)
Species	- Brown trout, rudd, pike, perch, roach, bream, eels
Season	- All year
Methods	- Fly fishing, spinning and worm fishing for trout. All lawful methods including ground bait and maggots for coarse fish
Bag Limit	- 2 pike per day
Size Limit	- Pike of 4 kg (8.8 lb) and over must be returned to the water
Other Restrictions	- If you do not hold a Game Rod Licence and Permit any trout taken must be returned gently to the water
Boats	- Fishing is permitted from non-mechanical boats only
Licence	- *Over 18* - Fisheries Conservancy Board Coarse Fishing Rod Licence (for coarse fish only) Fisheries Conservancy Board Game Fishing Rod Licence if fishing for trout
	- *Under 18* - None

Permit   - *Over 18* - Department of
Agriculture Coarse Fishing
Permit (for coarse fish only).
Department of Agriculture Game
Fishing Permit if fishing for trout
- *Under 18* - Department of
Agriculture Juvenile Game
Fishing Permit if fishing for trout.

Pike are the main quarry, with fish up to 9 kg (20 lb) caught in this lake. There is an abundance of perch and roach which tend to be small. Trout and bream are occasionally taken but are not the main interest of anglers. Caution should be exercised when boating as there are a number of shallow areas in the lough which are unmarked.

BOATS FOR HIRE:-

Carlton Fishing Centre, Belleek,
telephone: (03656) 31275
M Gilroy, Melvin Bar, Garrison,
telephone: (03656) 58380

HOW TO GET THERE

The lough is signposted from the main A47 Kesh to Belleek road.

119

River Roe

BINEVENAGH LAKE

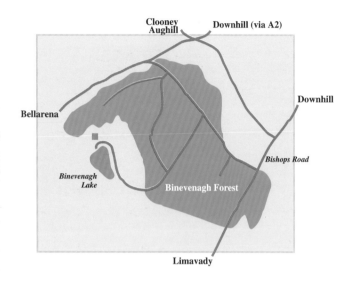

Nearest Town	- Limavady
Area	- 3.2 hectares (8 acres)
Species	- Rainbow trout
Season	- 1 February–31 December
Methods	- Fly fishing, spinning and worm fishing
Bag Limit	- 4 fish per rod per day
Size Limit	- Minimum takeable size 25.4 cm (10 inches)
Other Restrictions	- None
Boats	- Fishing from boats is not permitted
Licence	- *Over 18* - Foyle Fisheries Commission Game Fishing Rod Licence
	- *Under 18* - Foyle Fisheries Commission Juvenile Game Fishing Rod Licence
Permit	- *Over 18* - Department of Agriculture Game Fishing Permit
	- *Under 18* - Department of Agriculture Juvenile Game Fishing Permit.

This artificial lake commands a cliff-top situation set in a forest area and overlooking the picturesque Benone Strand. Due to increasing demand in this tourist area, the lake is stocked regularly with rainbow trout, some of which weigh 1–2.5 kg (2–5 lb).

HOW TO GET THERE

From Coleraine take the A2 to Downhill, turn left onto Bishops Road and continue for approximately 8 km (5 miles), turn right at the start of the forest and take the second forest entrance on the left.

From Limavady, take the coastal A2 road for approximately 3.2 km (2 miles). Fork right onto the B201 at Artikilly then left at the fork 1.6 km (1 mile) further on. Continue straight for a further 5.4 km (3½ miles), turn left at the end of the forest and take the second forest entrance on the left.

ANGLING SAFETY TIPS

FISHING IN A REMOTE AREA ?

- **WEAR PROPER CLOTHING**

- **LET SOMEONE KNOW WHERE YOU ARE**

- **TELL THEM WHAT TIME YOU EXPECT TO RETURN**

- **IF YOU ARE DELAYED – PHONE TO LET THEM KNOW**

COUNTY LONDONDERRY

RIVER ROE

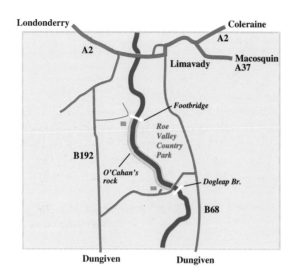

Nearest Town - Limavady

Length - 2 km (1¼ miles)

Species - Salmon and brown trout (including sea trout)

Season - 1 April–20 October

Methods - Fly fishing, spinning and bait fishing

Bag Limit - None

Size Limit - Fish under 25.4 cm (10 inches) must be returned unharmed to the water

Other Restrictions - Anglers should note that there are special requirements governing the methods of angling which may be used on the River Roe. Also, under certain conditions, fishing may be suspended at any time during the season. Full details about these requirements may be obtained from the Foyle Fisheries Commission, 8 Victoria Road, Londonderry BT47 2AB (telephone: (0504) 42100).

Angling is prohibited from and within 45 metres (50 yards) downstream of the weir known as O'Cahan's Rock

Boats - Fishing from boats is not permitted

Licence - *Over 18* - Foyle Fisheries Commission Game Fishing Rod Licence
- *Under 18* - Foyle Fisheries Commission Juvenile Game Fishing Rod Licence

Permit - *Over 18* - Department of Agriculture Game Fishing Permit
- *Under 18* - Department of Agriculture Juvenile Game Fishing Permit.

This salmon and trout fishery is situated in the beautiful Roe Valley Country Park near Limavady. A footbridge spans the river upstream of Givan's Weir giving anglers easy access to both banks.

HOW TO GET THERE

The river below O'Cahan's Rock is best fished from the left or northern bank. This is approached from the A2 just west of Limavady by the B69 south to Claudy, turning left after 1.2 km (¾ mile) onto the B192 to Dungiven. The road to the river is 1.2 km (¾ mile) further on the left (signposted).
The Dogleap area is best approached from the B68 Limavady-Dungiven road and is well signposted.

Enagh Lough

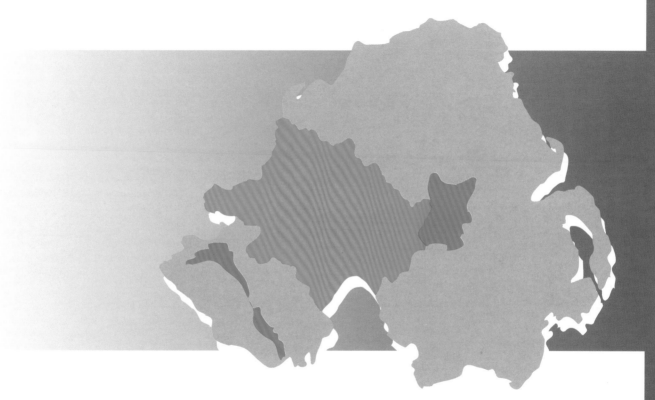

Loughs Bradan and Lee

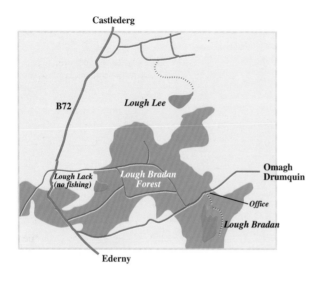

Note: *These are public reservoirs and care should be taken not to cause pollution.*

Nearest Town	- Drumquin
Area	- Bradan 24.3 hectares (60 acres) Lee 15 hectares (37 acres)
Species	- Brown trout
Season	- 1 March–20 October
Methods	- Fly fishing, spinning and bait fishing
Bag Limit	- 4 fish per rod per day
Size Limit	- Minimum takeable size 24.5 cm (10 inches)
Other Restrictions	- Fishing is not permitted from the weir on the north side of Lough Bradan
Boats	- Fishing from boats is not permitted
Licence	- *Over 18* - Foyle Fisheries Commission Game Fishing Rod Licence
	- *Under 18* - Foyle Fisheries Commission Juvenile Game Fishing Rod Licence
Permit	- *Over 18* - Department of Agriculture Game Fishing Permit
	- *Under 18* - Department of Agriculture Juvenile Game Fishing Permit.

LOUGH BRADAN

Lough Bradan is an upland lake situated in the scenic Lough Bradan forest 19.2 km (12 miles) west of Omagh. The lake is well stocked with brown trout which rise freely to the evening hatch of terrestrial flies. Bait fishing is more rewarding early in the season. Anglers are advised to use the east bank where a car-park is available close to the shore.

LOUGH LEE

Lough Lee is located in a wild and beautiful setting among the mountains of west Tyrone. In spite of its isolation, the walk from the nearest country road, less than 1.6 km (1 mile), takes only 20–25 minutes by the path staked out for anglers. This is sheep country and dogs are not welcome. All legal methods of angling are permitted.

Trout up to 1 kg (2 lb) weight are regularly taken from Lough Lee. The water is crystal clear and the distinctly marked trout bear no discolouration from the surrounding upland peat.

HOW TO GET THERE

Lough Bradan – from A5 (Omagh to Londonderry) take the B50, 1.6 km (1 mile) north of Omagh, travelling west for 11.2 km (7 miles), turn south by B84 for 0.8 km (½ mile), turning right (signposted) westwards for 6.4 km (4 miles).

From B72 (Castlederg to Ederny) 6.4 km (4 miles) north of Ederny turn east at signpost to Drumquin 4 km (2½ miles).

Lough Lee – from the B50 (Omagh to Castlederg via Drumquin) turn west at the signpost 8 km (5 miles) north of Drumquin 4.8 km (3 miles) south of Castlederg and continue for 2.8 km (1¾ miles) to the sign at the copse at Clare Lodge. Turn south for 2.4 km (1½ miles) to the limit of the surfaced country road.

From the B72 (Ederny to Castlederg), travel east as signposted to the copse at Clare Lodge, turn south to the end of the country road – 6.4 km (4½ miles).

COUNTY TYRONE

BRANTRY LOUGH

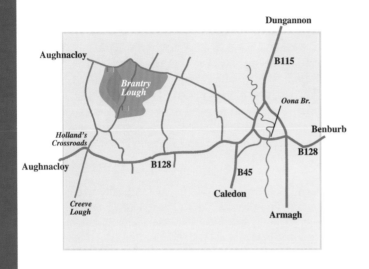

Nearest Town	- Benburb
Area	- 24.3 hectares (60 acres)
Species	- Brown trout
Season	- 1 March–31 October
Methods	- Fly fishing only from boat and shore
Bag Limit	- 4 fish per rod per day
Size Limit	- Minimum takeable size 25.4 cm (10 inches)
Other Restrictions	- None
Boats	- Fishing is permitted from non-mechanical boats only
Licence	- *Over 18* - Fisheries Conservancy Board Game Fishing Rod Licence
	- *Under 18* - None
Permit	- *Over 18* - Department of Agriculture Game Fishing Permit
	- *Under 18* - Department of Agriculture Juvenile Game Fishing Permit.

This is another popular lake providing high class brown trout fishing.

A surfaced path surrounds the lake and angling stands have been provided. There is a soft boggy pocket in the bay at the south-east corner near the car-park and anglers should exercise great care when wading in this area.

HOW TO GET THERE

From Belfast to the end of the M1 continuing on the Dungannon by-pass for approximately 0.4 km (¼ mile) past the service area. Turn left onto the B45 to Caledon travelling through Eglish, turning right at the crossroads just over the Oona Bridge from where the lake is signposted.

From Aughnacloy take the B128 Benburb road for 7.2 km (4½ miles). Turn left at Holland's Crossroads where the lake is indicated by a signpost.

COUNTY TYRONE

LOUGH CREEVE

(Designated coarse fishery)

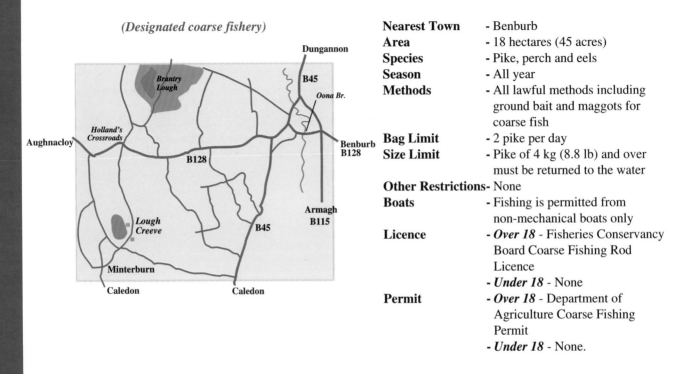

Nearest Town	- Benburb
Area	- 18 hectares (45 acres)
Species	- Pike, perch and eels
Season	- All year
Methods	- All lawful methods including ground bait and maggots for coarse fish
Bag Limit	- 2 pike per day
Size Limit	- Pike of 4 kg (8.8 lb) and over must be returned to the water
Other Restrictions	- None
Boats	- Fishing is permitted from non-mechanical boats only
Licence	- *Over 18* - Fisheries Conservancy Board Coarse Fishing Rod Licence
	- *Under 18* - None
Permit	- *Over 18* - Department of Agriculture Coarse Fishing Permit
	- *Under 18* - None.

132

Creeve is the sister lake of Bantry and is situated south of the Aughnacloy-Benburb road. A hardcore path surrounds the lake and gives easy access to the fishing stands provided. There is a background of deciduous trees which supply shade to the lake and car-parks.

Scientific examination has shown Creeve to be very productive, with a perch growth rate exceeding all other Irish waters. A 0.6 kg (1 lb 5 oz) perch has been taken from this lake and the heaviest pike reported was 16.9 kg (35 lb) and measured 109 cm (3 ft 7 in) in length.

Not far from these loughs is Parkanaur Forest Park, where there is a display of machines used in the development of Ulster's forests. There is also a nature trail.

Car-park, toilets, caravan and camping facilities are all available in the forest park.

HOW TO GET THERE

From Caledon turn left for Minterburn off the Dungannon B45 road a short distance from Caledon. Turn right at Minterburn towards Lough Creeve.

From Aughnacloy take the B128 Benburb road for 7.2 km (4½ miles), turn right at Holland's Crossroads where the lough is indicated by a sign.

COUNTY TYRONE

133

ENAGH LOUGH

(Designated coarse fishery)

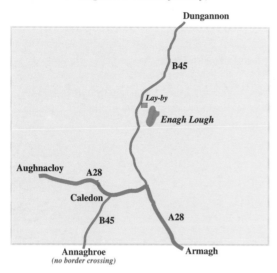

Nearest Town	- Caledon
Area	- 5.3 hectares (13 acres)
Species	- Pike, perch, eels and bream
Season	- All year
Methods	- All lawful methods including ground bait and maggots
Bag Limit	- 2 pike per day
Size Limit	- Pike of 4 kg (8.8 lb) and over must be returned to the water
Other Restrictions	- None
Boats	- Fishing from boats is not permitted
Licence	- *Over 18* - Fisheries Conservancy Board Coarse Fishing Rod Licence
	- *Under 18* - None
Permit	- *Over 18* - Department of Agriculture Coarse Fishing Permit
	- *Under 18* - None.

Enagh Lough lies at the side of the main Caledon-Dungannon road about 1.6 km (1 mile) from Caledon. The side nearest the road has been developed for angling and a small car-park, hardcore path and fishing stands have been provided.

This water has a good name for big pike, and fish in the 7–9 kg (15–20 lb) class have been caught in the past as well as many smaller pike and bream. Some tench may also be present.

HOW TO GET THERE

From Caledon take the B45 Dungannon road for approximately 1.6 km (1 mile) and the lough is on your right.

From Dungannon travel towards Caledon on the B45 for about 17.7 km (11 miles) and the lough is on your left.

Coarse fishing on Enagh Lough

COUNTY TYRONE

MOOR LOUGH AND LOUGH ASH

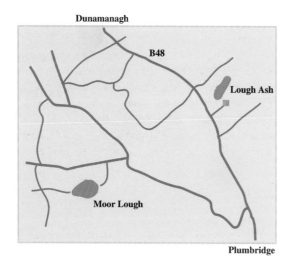

Nearest Town	- Dunamanagh
Area	- Moor Lough 16.2 hectares (40 acres) Lough Ash 15.3 hectares (38 acres)
Species	- Brown trout
Season	- 1 March–20 October
Methods	- Fly fishing, spinning and bait fishing
Bag Limit	- 4 fish per rod per day
Size Limit	- Minimum takeable size 25.4 cm (10 inches)
Other Restrictions	- None
Boats	- Fishing from boats is not permitted
Licence	- *Over 18* - Foyle Fisheries Commission Game Fishing Rod Licence
	- *Under 18* - Foyle Fisheries Commission Juvenile Game Fishing Rod Licence
Permit	- *Over 18* - Department of Agriculture Game Fishing Permit
	- *Under 18* - Department of Agriculture Juvenile Game Fishing Permit.

MOOR LOUGH

Situated in mountainous countryside, Moor Lough and the adjoining area are developed as an amenity area. The surrounding gravel road gives easy access to all the shoreline. Disabled anglers would find this water particularly accessible.

HOW TO GET THERE

From Belfast via the A6 by Dungiven, taking the B49 through Claudy to Dunamanagh. Head south for about 90 metres (100 yards) by the B48 towards Plumbridge, turning right to Altishane. Cross the Silverbrook Bridge 3.2 km (2 miles) out and turn left for another 1.6 km (1 mile) to Devine's public house. Turn right for 2 km (1¼ miles) over the moor, then left for 450 metres (500 yards) and left again by the gravel road to the lake.

From Strabane travel north by the A5 towards Londonderry, turning right 3.2 km (2 miles) out of Strabane towards Dunamanagh B49. Turn right again in Artigarvan village for 6.4 km (4 miles) through Glenmornan, then right for 450 metres (500 yards) and left by the road to the lake.

Road signs are provided from Lough Ash.

LOUGH ASH

Lough Ash is situated in the picturesque countryside of Dunamanagh. The lake is stocked exclusively with brown trout. Over the past two years larger trout were used for stocking with the view to providing the angler with more rewarding catches. Because of the dangerous bank, the western shore is closed to anglers and the short eastern end is inaccessible because of reeds. The northern and southern shores supply spacious wading areas. Perimeter stiles and footbridges from the car-park give unrestricted access to the fishing areas.

HOW TO GET THERE

From Belfast to Dungiven, taking the B49 through Claudy and Dunamanagh. Turn left on the B48 to Plumbridge. The signposted entrance to the car-park is on the left 4.8 km (3 miles) from Dunamanagh.

RIVER MOURNE

(Managed by Sion Mills Angling Club)

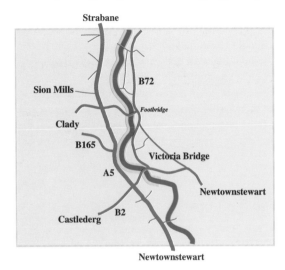

Strabane
B72
Sion Mills
Footbridge
Clady
B165
Victoria Bridge
A5
Newtownstewart
B2
Castlederg

Newtownstewart

Note: Anglers should note that angling may be suspended at any time during the season when certain conditions prevail. Full details may be obtained from the Foyle Fisheries Commission, 8 Victoria Road, Londonderry (telephone: (0504) 42100).

Nearest Town	- Sion Mills
Length	- 6.4 km (4 miles)
Species	- Salmon and brown trout (including sea trout)
Season	- 1 April–20 October
Methods	- Fly fishing, spinning and bait fishing (floats not permitted)
Bag Limit	- None
Size Limit	- None
Other Restrictions	- Fishing is not permitted within 64 metres (58½ yards) downstream of Sion Weir on the left or western bank
Boats	- Fishing from boats is not permitted
Licence	- *Over 18* - Foyle Fisheries Commission Game Fishing Rod Licence
	- *Under 18* - Foyle Fisheries Commission Juvenile Game Fishing Rod Licence
Permit	- *Over 18* - Sion Mills Angling Club Day Ticket
	- *Under 18* - Sion Mills Angling Club Day Ticket.

Under an agreement with the Department, Sion Mills Angling Club manages the fishing rights in those parts of the River Mourne previously managed by the Department. They are operated in conjunction with the Sion Mills Angling Club stretches as a single fishery. A total of 30 day tickets is available daily, free of charge, to holders of Department of Agriculture Adult or Juvenile Game Season Permits. These may be obtained on production of a valid Department Permit from:-

Timothy Kee, Mourne Bar, Victoria Bridge,
Co Tyrone, telephone: Sion Mills (06626) 58243
– 10 tickets daily.

Mark Gough, 6 New Street, Sion Mills – 20 tickets daily.

Day tickets are also available to other anglers on payment of a day ticket charge. Details of, for example, the extent of the fishery and access points are available from day ticket sellers.

HOW TO GET THERE

From Belfast to the end of the M1, taking the Dungannon by-pass to Ballygawley and the A5 to Omagh continuing on the A5 through Newtownstewart to Victoria Bridge and Sion Mills.

From Londonderry on the A5 through Strabane to Sion Mills.

COUNTY TYRONE

RIVER STRULE

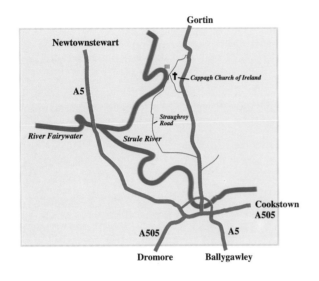

Nearest Town	- Omagh
Length	- Approximately 2.4 km (1½ miles)
Species	- Roach, eels (game fish must not be taken)
Season	- All year except between 1 July and 20 October (coarse fishing competitions may be allowed in the close season by special arrangement with the Department)
Methods	- All lawful methods including ground bait and maggots
Bag Limit	- None
Size Limit	- None
Other Restrictions	- Maximum line breaking strain of 2 kg (4.4 lb). Maximum hook size 12. Any game fish accidentally captured must be returned unharmed to the water
Boats	- Fishing from boats is not permitted

Licence	- None
Permit	- *Over 18* - Department of Agriculture Coarse Fishing Permit
	- *Under 18* - None.

By arrangement with Omagh Anglers' Association, the Department controls the coarse fishing (that is, all freshwater fish except salmon and trout) on a stretch of the River Strule extending downstream on the right (east) bank only from the junction with the Fairywater. The entrance and car-park are at the downstream end which is near Cappagh Church of Ireland.

HOW TO GET THERE

Take the B4 Gortin Road from Omagh for 2.8 km (1¾ miles). Turn left at Coronation Cottages and left again at Cappagh Church of Ireland.

COUNTY TYRONE

WHITE LOUGH

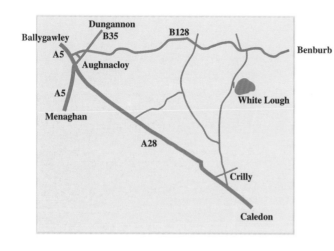

Nearest Town	- Aughnacloy
Area	- 9.3 hectares (23 acres)
Species	- Rainbow trout
Season	- 1 February–31 December
Methods	- Fly fishing, spinning and worm fishing. Fly fishing only from boats
Bag Limit	- 4 fish per rod per day
Size Limit	- Minimum takeable size 24.5 cm (10 inches)
Other Restrictions	- None
Boats	- Fishing is permitted from non-mechanical boats only
Licence	- *Over 18* - Fisheries Conservancy Board Game Fishing Rod Licence
	- *Under 18* - None
Permit	- *Over 18* - Department of Agriculture Game Fishing Permit
	- *Under 18* - Department of Agriculture Juvenile Game Fishing Permit.

White Lough is a most attractive lough in a pleasant setting by Rehaghy Mountain, near Aughnacloy. There is a surfaced path from the adjoining county road around the entire shoreline and numerous fishing stands have been provided. Since it was designated as a rainbow trout fishery, it has proved very popular with anglers.

Visitors may enjoy a quiet walk around the shore provided no annoyance is caused to the adjoining landowners. Small boats are permitted but power-boating is not allowed.

HOW TO GET THERE

From Aughnacloy via the main road to Caledon A28 to Crilly (3.2 km (2 miles) from Aughnacloy); turn left then fork right after 0.4 km (¼ mile) at McClure's shop.

From Aughnacloy by the B128 to Benburb turn right at the second (Rehaghy) crossroads 3.2 km (2 miles) out (both signposted).

Spinning for trout on White Lough

COUNTY TYRONE

143

ANGLING CLUB WATERS AVAILABLE TO THE PUBLIC

There are a large number of popular angling clubs throughout Northern Ireland offering mostly brown or rainbow trout fishing on lakes and rivers. Some salmon fishing is also available. The following clubs sell day tickets to non-club members. Prices are liable to alteration, and so are not quoted. Tickets are available from the outlets listed with each club.

Additional conditions may be imposed by the club, and bag limits, size limits and angling methods should be checked before you start to fish.

You do not need a Department of Agriculture Permit to fish these waters, but you do need a Fisheries Conservancy Board or Foyle Fisheries Commission Rod Licence.

AGIVEY ANGLERS ASSOCIATION

Waters - Total length of Agivey and Wee Agivey Rivers and their tributaries
Nearest town - Garvagh
Species - Salmon and brown trout
Season - 1 March to 30 September
Methods - Fly fishing, spinning and worm fishing. Prawns, shrimps and maggots are not permitted
Day tickets - 12 tickets are available each day from Mrs J McCann, 162 Agivey Road, Aghadowey (for Agivey River) or Mr Bert Atkins, Coleraine Road, Garvagh (for Wee Agivey).

ARMAGH ANGLING CLUB

Waters - Lowry's, Tullnawood, Seagaghan and Shaw's Lakes
Nearest towns - Markethill and Armagh
Species - Brown and rainbow trout
Bag limit - 6 fish per day
Size limit - Fish of 27.5 cm (11 inches) or less must be returned to the water
Methods - Shaw's Lake - fly fishing only Others - fly fishing, spinning and worm fishing
Day tickets - Available from Texaco Service Station, Moy Road, Armagh or at the gate to Shaw's Lake.

BALLYNURE ANGLING CLUB

Waters - Two stretches of the Sixmile River
    (i) Doagh Bridge to Milltown Bridge
    (ii) War Memorial Park to Ballynure
Nearest towns - Ballynure and Ballyclare
Species - Brown trout
Season - 1 March to 31 October
Methods - Fly fishing only from Doagh Bridge to Milltown Bridge. All legal methods from War Memorial Park to Ballynure
Bag limit - 4 fish per day
Size limit - Fish under 25.4 cm (10 inches) must be returned to the water
Day tickets - Available from Doagh Service Station; Wilson's Garage, Milltown; 'Seven Days'; Benny Craig's Hardware Store, Main Street, Ballyclare.

BALLINDERRY BRIDGE ANGLING CLUB

Waters - Ballinderry River, Co Tyrone from Birch Wood near Coagh to Lough Neagh
Nearest town - Coagh
Species - Brown trout (dollaghan)
Methods - All legal methods permitted
Day tickets - Available from McCrystal's Filling Station, Ballinderry Bridge Road, Coagh.

BANBRIDGE ANGLING CLUB

Waters - Upper Bann River from Hazelbank Weir, Lenaderg to Katesbridge
Nearest town - Banbridge
Species - Brown trout, grilse and some coarse fish
Season - 1 March to 31 October
Methods - All legal methods except maggot fishing
Bag limit - 4 fish per day
Size limit - Fish under 25.4 cm (10 inches) must be returned to the water
Day tickets - 40 day tickets per day are available from Messrs Coburns Ltd, Scarva Street, Banbridge and Angler's Rest, Corbett, Katesbridge.

BELFAST ANGLERS ASSOCIATION

Waters - Lough Island Reavey, Upper Holywood Reservoir and Creighton's Green Reservoir
Nearest towns - Castlewellan, Belfast, Holywood
Species - Brown trout
Season - 1 April to 30 September
Methods - Fly fishing only
Bag limit - 3 fish per day

Size limit - All fish under 30 cm (12 inches) must be returned to the water

Other restrictions - No Sunday fishing

Day tickets - 6 tickets for Lough Island Reavey are available from Mr A McNeilly, 177 Lacken Road, Kilcoo, Newry, telephone: (08206) 50537. Two tickets are available for each of the others from Mr Edmond Herron, Herron's Newsagency, 22 Church Street, Holywood, telephone: (0232) 422245.

BLACKISTON HOUSTON ESTATE

Waters - Owenkillew and Owenreagh

Species - Salmon, sea trout, brown trout

Season - 1 April to 10/20 October

Methods - Fly fishing

Day tickets - Available from Mr Vic Betteridge, telephone: (06626) 48346 or Mr John Patterson, telephone: (06626) 48207.

Entrance is via the white gates to the Beltrim Estate at the crossroads in Gortin, that is, where the B48 (Plumbridge to Omagh) and B46 (Sixmilecross to Newtownstewart) meet.

CLADY AND DISTRICT ANGLING CLUB

Water - Clady River and tributaries

Nearest town - Portglenone

Species - Salmon and brown trout

Season - 1 March to 31 October

Methods - Fly only on certain stretches. No shrimp, float or maggot fishing

Day tickets - Available from Weir's, Clady Road, Portglenone; Moira's shop, Portglenone; Clady Post Office, Glenone Road, Clady.

COLERAINE ANGLERS ASSOCIATION

Waters - Ballinreese Reservoir and River Ree

Nearest towns - Coleraine, Ballymoney

Species - Brown trout and occasional grilse and sea trout

Day tickets - Available from the Hon Treasurer, Mr A F White, 83 Central Avenue, Portstewart.

CRUMLIN ANGLING CLUB

Water - Crumlin River
Nearest town - Crumlin
Species - Brown trout, and dollaghan in the lower reaches in September–October
Methods - All legal methods
Bag limit - 8 fish
Size limit - All fish under 24.5 cm (10 inches) must be returned to the water
Day tickets - Day tickets or an annual permit are available from Fur, Feather & Fin Tackle Shop, Mill Road, Crumlin.

DOAGH ANGLING CLUB

Water - Doagh Burn
Nearest town - Doagh
Species - Brown trout
Season - 1 March to 31 October
Methods - Fly fishing only
Bag limit - 4 fish
Size limit - All fish under 23 cm (9 inches) must be returned to the water
Day tickets - Available from W Duddy, Newsagent, Main Street, Doagh.

DROMORE ANGLING CLUB

Water - River Lagan from the Dromore side of the Guildhall Estate to Moydalgan, Dromara
Nearest towns - Dromore, Dromara
Species - Brown trout
Season - 1 March to 30 September
Methods - Mainly fly with some worm fishing, but no spinning and no maggots
Bag limit - 4 fish per day
Size limit - All fish under 25 cm (10 inches) must be returned to the water
Day tickets - Available from J McCracken, Confectioners, Gallows Street, Dromore.

DUNGIVEN ANGLERS CLUB

Water - River Roe from Ross Mill to Bovevagh Bridge
Species - Salmon and sea trout
Season - 1 April to 20 October
Day tickets - Available from Patsy McGuigan, 24 Station Road, Dungiven; Mrs Wilson, Bovevagh Post Office, Bovevagh, Dungiven.

River Faughan Anglers Association

Water - River Faughan
Nearest town - Londonderry
Species - Sea trout and salmon
Methods - Fly fishing only at night; fly fishing, spinning or worm fishing during the day
Day tickets - Available from Club Offices, 26 Carlisle Road, Londonderry.

Glenravel and Clough Angling Club

Waters - Clough River from Glarryford to Gaston's Bridge and Silverstream Fish Farm to Martinstown
Species - Trout with salmon and dollaghan from July
Season - 1 April to 31 October
Methods - All legal methods except no spinning before 1 July
Size limits - All fish under 24.5 cm (10 inches) must be returned to the water
Other restrictions - Fishing only between 8 am and dusk
Day tickets - Available from Ivan Linton, Maxol Garage, 318 Frosses Road, Glarryford or Spar Shop, Martinstown.

Glens Angling Club

Waters - Glendun River, Glenariff River, River Dall
Nearest towns - Cushendall and Glenariff
Species - Salmon and sea trout
Season - 1 June to 31 October
Methods - Fly fishing, spinning and worm fishing
Day tickets - Available from McAllister's Angling Shop, Waterfoot; Bay Hotel, Cushendun; Mrs McFetridge, 116 Dromara Road, Castle Green, Cushendun.

Gracehill, Galgorm and district Angling Club

Waters - River Maine - both banks downstream from Fenaghy House Estate boundary to where the Braid River enters the Maine and from this point the right hand bank adjoining J O'Rawe's farm.
Braid River from where it joins the Maine to Tullygarley Bridge, on the Castle Estate bank only
Nearest town - Ballymena
Species - Brown trout and salmon
Season - 1 March to 31 October
Methods - All legal methods except no spinning until 1 August.

Bag limit - 6 fish per day
Size limit - All fish under 25.4 cm (10 inches) must be returned to the water
Other restrictions - No Sunday fishing
Day tickets - 6 day tickets are available from Galgorm Post Office.

IVEAGH ANGLING CLUB

Waters - River Lagan (see page 80).

KELLS AND CONNOR ANGLING CLUB

Waters - River Kells from Pigtail Weir to the Maine River and Glenwherry River
Species - Brown trout with some late salmon and dollaghan
Season - 1 March to 31 October
Methods - Fly fishing, spinning and worm fishing from 1 August to 31 October and fly fishing only 1 March to 31 July
Bag limit - 6 fish per day
Size limit - All fish under 25.4 cm (10 inches) must be returned to the water
Other restrictions - No Sunday fishing
Day tickets - Available from Duncan's Filling Station, Kells.

KILDRESS ANGLING CLUB

Waters - Part of Ballinderry River, Co Tyrone (see details on day ticket)
Nearest town - Cookstown
Species - Brown trout (dollaghan)
Methods - All legal methods
Day tickets - 6 tickets per day Monday to Saturday inclusive are available from Drum Manor Filling Station.

KILKEEL ANGLING CLUB

Waters - Kilkeel and Whitewater Rivers
Species - Brown trout, sea trout, salmon
Methods - All lawful methods except maggots
Other restrictions - No Sunday fishing
The Club's waters do not extend into the Mourne Park Demesne
Day tickets - 6 day tickets available from S R Nicholson, Hardware Merchant, The Square, Kilkeel; Trevor Graham's Sports Shop, Kilkeel.

MAINE ANGLING CLUB

Water   - River Maine from above Cullybackey to Dunminning Bridge (see page 48).

MOYOLA AND DISTRICT ANGLING CLUB

Waters   - Moyola River and tributaries
Nearest towns - Castledawson, Draperstown, Maghera, Magherafelt
Species   - Brown trout, salmon
Season   - 1 March to 30 September
Size limit   - All fish under 24.5 cm (10 inches) must be returned to the water
Other restrictions - Landowners' permission may be required for access
Day tickets   - Available from G Ewing's Confectionery Shop, 41 Main Street, Castledawson, telephone: (0648) 68517; H Heuston's Tackle Shop, 55 Main Street, Castledawson, telephone: (0648) 68282; Gilbert Crawford, Main Street, Maghera, telephone: (0648) 42369.

NEWRY AND DISTRICT ANGLING CLUB

Water   - Clanrye River, Grinan Lake, McCourts Lake
Species   - Brown trout with rainbow trout in Grinan Lake
Methods   - Fly fishing, spinning and worm fishing except certain areas which are marked fly fishing only
Bag limit   - 3 fish
Size limit   - All fish under 28 cm (11 inches) must be returned to the water
Day tickets   - Available from Mrs E McAlinden, 12 Lisgullion Park, Armagh Road, Newry.

OMAGH ANGLERS' ASSOCIATION

Waters   - The whole of the River Strule and stretches of the Camowen, Drumragh and Owenkillew Rivers
Nearest towns - Newtownstewart, Omagh
Species   - Salmon, sea trout, brown trout, some coarse fish
Methods   - All legal methods but ground bait, maggots, prawns and shrimps are not permitted
Day tickets   - Available from C A Anderson & Co, Market Street, Omagh; Chism Fishing Tackle, Bridge Street, Omagh; D Campbell, Mill Street, Newtownstewart; J Graham, 6 Bessie Bell Court, Newtownstewart.

RANDALSTOWN ANGLING CLUB

Water - River Maine from Randalstown Road Bridge to Andraid Ford
Nearest town - Randalstown
Species - Trout, salmon and dollaghan
Methods - All legal methods except maggots
Bag limit - 4 fish per day
Size limit - All fish under 25.4 cm (10 inches) must be returned to the water
Other restrictions - No Sunday fishing
Day tickets - Available from Spence Brothers, 32 New Street, Randalstown; New Street Filling Station, New Street, Randalstown; VG Store, 51 Slaght Street, Ballymena.

RATHFRILAND ANGLING CLUB

Water - Part of the Upper Bann
Nearest town - Rathfriland
Species - Brown trout and salmon
Methods - All lawful methods
Bag limit - 6 brown trout or 3 salmon.
Day tickets - 10 tickets per day are available from W R Trimble, 25 Downpatrick Street, Rathfriland; or F McNeill, 64 Cross Heights, Rathfriland.

SHIMNA ANGLING CLUB

Water - Part of the Shimna River
Nearest town - Newcastle
Species - Sea trout and salmon
Methods - Fly fishing only from 1 March to 30 June and all legal methods for game fish 1 July to 15 October
Bag limit - 6 fish per day
Size limit - All fish under 25.4 cm (10 inches) must be returned to the water
Day tickets - 4 daily and 6 weekly tickets are available from Four Seasons, 47 Main Street, Newcastle.

WARRENPOINT, ROSTREVOR AND DISTRICT ANGLING CLUB

Waters - The Mill Dam, Grinan Road, Warrenpoint and the Waterworks, Burren Road, Warrenpoint
Species - Trout
Day tickets - Available from First Choice Confectionery Shop, 4 Quay Street, Warrenpoint, telephone: (06937) 72702.

WOODBURN GAME ANGLING ASSOCIATION

Waters - Dorisland Reservoir

Nearest town - Carrickfergus

Methods - Fly fishing only

Other restrictions - Access via car-park on Knockagh Road only

Day tickets - 10 day tickets available from Gault's Grocery Shop, Woodburn Corner, telephone: (09603) 62281.

PRIVATE FISHERIES AVAILABLE TO THE PUBLIC

The number of private put-and-take fisheries in Northern Ireland is increasing. These small lakes may be natural or artificial and are well stocked, promising good bags for the visiting angler. Tuition is available at nearly all of these fisheries. Most are also designated as Rainbow Trout Fisheries and so are open all year round.

You do not need a Department of Agriculture Fishing Permit to fish these waters, but you do need a Fisheries Conservancy Board or Foyle Fisheries Commission Rod Licence.

Charges and other information are available from the individual fisheries concerned.

ASH COTTAGE FISHERY

Address - Ash Cottage, 42 Ballyblack Road, Newtownards, Co Down BT22 2AZ
Telephone - (0247) 862400
Season - Open all year
Opening times - 9 am to 10 pm or dusk, whichever is the earlier
Species - Rainbow trout
Methods - Fly fishing only
Bag limit - None
Tuition - Tuition is available
Other facilities - Meals and sandwiches, toilets, rest room, etc.

BRIDGEWATER FISHERY

Address - 93 Windmill Road, Donaghadee, Co Down, BT21 0NQ
Telephone - (0247) 883348
Season - Open all year
Opening times - 9 am to 10 pm
Species - Rainbow trout
Methods - Fly fishing only
Bag limit - Depends on day ticket
Tuition - Tuition is available
Other facilities - Fisherman's Lodge Tea Room, toilets, farmhouse bed and breakfast accommodation.

THE CORNMILL FISHERY

Address - 25 Shanes Hill Road, Kilwaughter, Larne, Co Antrim, BT40 2PA
Telephone - (0574) 273186 and (0850) 255691
Season - Open all year
Opening times - 9 am to 10 pm or dusk, whichever is earlier
Species - Rainbow trout
Bag limit - Catch and release only
Methods - Fly fishing only
Tuition - Tuition is available on Saturday and Sunday if booked in advance
Other facilities - Barbecue and picnic area.

CRANOGUE FISHERY

Address - Cranogue House, 15 Toberdoney Road, Liscolman, Ballymoney, Co Antrim, BT53 8EA
Telephone - (02657) 41272
Season - Open all year
Opening times - 9 am to 10 pm
Species - Rainbow trout
Methods - Fly fishing and lures
Bag limit - 4 fish on a half-day ticket
Tuition - Tuition is available
Other facilities - Anglers' hut and toilets.

THE DAIRY FISHERY

Address - 179A Belfast Road, Ballynahinch, Co Down, BT24 8UR
Telephone - (0238) 563380
Season - Open all year
Opening times - Tuesday to Friday 9 am to 5.30 pm Saturday and Sunday 9 am to 5 pm
Species - Rainbow trout
Methods - Fly fishing only except on Wednesdays when worm fishing is permitted
Bag limit - 3 on a half-day ticket
Tuition - Tuition is available
Other facilities - Part of the fishery is ideal for disabled anglers. Club room with tea, coffee and hot snacks, tackle shop.

HAZELDEN FISHERY

Address - 134 Lough Fea Road, Cookstown, Co Tyrone, BT80 9ST
Telephone - (06487) 61575
Season - Open all year
Opening times - Monday to Saturday 8.30 am to dusk
Species - Rainbow trout
Methods - Fly fishing only
Bag limit - 4 fish

Parklake Fishery

Address - Dungannon Park, Moy Road, Dungannon, Co Tyrone
Telephone - (08687) 27327
Season - Open all year
Opening times - Monday to Saturday 8.30 am to dusk, Sunday 9 am to dusk
Species - Rainbow trout
Methods - Fly fishing only from boat, bank and fishing stands
Bag limit - 2–5 fish, depending on the ticket purchased
Tuition - Tuition is available by appointment
Other facilities - Shop, scenic walks, children's play area, toilet facilities (including for the disabled), putting green, target golf, barbecue area, fishing stands and car-parking.

Springwell Fishery

Address - 15 Drumsamney Road, Tobermore, Magherafelt, Co Londonderry, BT45 5QX
Telephone - (0648) 43728/42647
Season - Open all year
Opening times - Tuesday to Sunday 10 am to 8 pm
Species - Rainbow trout
Methods - Fly fishing only
Tuition - Tuition is available
Other facilities - Cross-country course, riding-school with pony-trekking, refreshments, rod hire.

Straid Fishery

Address - Castletown Road, Ballynure, Ballyclare, Co Antrim BT39 3PU
Telephone - (0960) 340099
Season - Open all year, except Christmas Day
Opening times - 9 am to dusk or 11 pm, whichever is the earlier
Species - Rainbow trout
Methods - Fly fishing only
Bag limit - Depends on day ticket
Tuition - Tuition is available on Saturday and Sunday mornings
Other facilities - Toilets, free tea and coffee, confectionery, tackle and flies, boats for hire, car-parking.

TILDARG FISHERY

Address - 35 Tildarg Road, Tildarg, Ballyclare, Co Antrim, BT39 9JU

Telephone - (0960) 340604 or 322216

Season - Open all year except Christmas Day

Opening times - 9 am to dusk

Species - Rainbow trout

Methods - Fly fishing only

Bag limit - Depends on day ticket

Other facilities - Lodge with tea-room, kitchen, fishing tackle, toilets and disabled anglers' boat.

Date	Water	Species	Method	Weight

Catch Record

Date	Water	Species	Method	Weight

Date	Water	Species	Method	Weight

 **HMSO**

HMSO publications are available from:

HMSO Publications Centre
(Mail and telephone orders only)
PO Box 276, London SW8 5DT
Telephone orders 071-873 9090
General enquiries 071-837 0011
(queuing system in operation for both numbers)
Fax orders 071-873 8200

HMSO Bookshops
16 Arthur Street, Belfast BT1 4DG
0232-238451 Fax: 0232-235401
49 High Holborn, London WC1V 6HB
071-837 0011 Fax: 071-837 *(counter service only)*
285 Broad Street, Birmingham B1 2HE
021-643 3740 Fax: 021-643 6510
33 Wine Street, Bristol BS1 2BQ
0272-264306 Fax: 0272-294515
9-12 Princess Street, Manchester M60 8AS
061-834 7201 Fax: 061-883 0634
71 Lothian Road, Edinburgh EH3 9AZ
031-228 4181 Fax: 031-229 2734

HMSO's Accredited Agents
(see Yellow Pages)
And through good booksellers